War and Ethics

Think Now

Think Now is a brand new series of stimulating and accessible books examining key contemporary social issues from a philosophical perspective. Written by experts in philosophy, these books offer sophisticated and provocative yet engaging writing on political and cultural themes of genuine concern to the educated reader.

The Ethics of Climate Change, James Garvey
Identity Crisis, Jeremy Stangroom
War and Ethics, Nicholas Fotion
Terrorism, Nicholas Fotion, Boris Kashnikov and Joanne K. Lekea

Series Editors:
James Garvey is Secretary of The Royal Institute of Philosophy and author of *The Twenty Greatest Philosophy Books* (Continuum)
Jeremy Stangroom is co-editor, with Julian Baggini, of *The Philosophers' Magazine and co-author of Why Truth Matters, What philosophers Think and Great Thinkers A–Z* (all Continuum).

War and Ethics

A New Just War Theory

Nicholas Fotion

continuum

Continuum International Publishing Group
The Tower Building
11 York Road
London
SE1 7NX

80 Maiden Lane
Suite 704
New York
NY 10038

www.continuumbooks.com

First published 2007

British Library Cataloguing-in-Publication Data
A catalogue record for this book is available from the British Library.

Library of Congress Cataloging-in-Publication Data
Fotion N.
War and ethics : a new just war theory / Nicholas Fotion.
p. cm.
Includes bibliographical references and index.
ISBN-13: 978-0-8264-9260-9
ISBN-10: 0-8264-9260-6
ISBN-13: 978-0-8264-9259-3 (alk. paper)
ISBN-10: 0-8264-9259-2 (alk. paper)
1. War—Moral and ethical aspects. 2. Just war doctrine. I. Title.

U22.F65 2007
172'.42—dc22

2007007726

Typeset by Servis Filmsetting Ltd, Manchester
Printed and bound in Great Britain by Ashford Colour Press Ltd, Gosport, Hampshire

Contents

Preface

In its present form, Just War Theory has been with us for several centuries. Its purpose has been, and still is, to give guidance when war is imminent. It is supposed to help nations decide whether it is morally (ethically) proper to go to war. Once a war starts, its purpose is also to give guidance as to whether certain ways of fighting are ethical or not.

The theory has been a disappointment to some. Among other things, they complain that it is not used enough, or that it is used insincerely, or that it actually does more harm that good when used and is, in any case, too vague to do much good. Yet the theory has its supporters. These followers find that it does the work it is supposed to do and does it in a wide variety of circumstances.

This disagreement between critics and followers suggests that it is time to reassess the theory. But reassessment is needed for other reasons as well. Technology, especially since World War II, has changed the nature of war. Politics has also changed. More than in the past, wars are not just between two or more nations but between nations and non-nation groups (i.e., rebels, insurgents, terrorists, etc.). Given these changes, the question that comes to mind is: should Just War Theory change so as to correspond to the changes of modern war? If it changes, how should it change? Should the changes be radical so that, in fact, the theory is mostly or totally abandoned? Should it be replaced by some other theory (such as pacifism) or, more fundamentally, should it be replaced by no theory at all? Or, should the changes be more modest?

These are the questions addressed in this book. The approach in answering them starts by placing Just War Theory in a larger theoretical context (Chapter 1) and then by giving an account of the theory as we know it today (Chapter 2). After taking a preliminary look at some objections to the theory (Chapter 3), the book moves to a series of case studies that show the theory at work (Chapters 4 and 5). Following these case studies, more cases are discussed, but there is a gradual move in the direction of accepting certain important changes to the theory (Chapters 6–8). The changes are then consolidated into a (new) modified just war theory that, surprisingly, forms not just one theory but two versions of one theory (Chapter 9). The first version deals with so-called regular wars (between nations) and the second with irregular wars (usually between a nation and a non-nation group). Once the Twin Just War Theory is developed, criticisms of Just War Theory in general and the Twin Theory in particular are assessed (Chapters 10 and 11). The book ends with a look back at what has and has not been accomplished (Chapter 12).

1 Introduction

UNIVERSAL PRINCIPLES

Some principles of ethics have a special status. They are thought to be unquestionably and universally true or correct. As will become evident shortly, that these principles have this status is clear enough. Why they have this status is another matter. Some say that they are true or correct by revelation, others tell us that they have this status by the light of reason. Still others appeal to utility, to natural rights, or appeal to ideals associated with the human virtues.

In this study, the why-question will be largely sidestepped. It is not important that it be answered. What is important is simply that there are some principles that are taken as having universal or almost universal status. But then, one wants to ask: what are these principles or rules?[1] Not surprisingly, they are ones we have all known about since we were children. Different individuals and different cultures express them differently. This makes it difficult to present a list that is satisfactory to all. But given some slack, the following is accepted by most.

1. Do not kill others.
2. Do not kill yourself.
3. Do what you can to minimize the suffering of others.
4. Do not harm others or yourself.
5. Help others when you can.

6. Do not deceive others (i.e., do not lie, withhold relevant information, exaggerate, etc.).
7. Keep your promises.
8. Treat others fairly (with justice).
9. Do not take what is not yours (do not steal).[2]

Perhaps other principles could, or should, be added to the list. But for the present purposes of understanding the work these kinds of principles do and do not do in our thinking, the list is long enough.

ABSOLUTE AND PRESUMPTIVE PRINCIPLES

It should be noted at the outset that these principles can be treated in one of two radically different ways. One way is as *absolute* universal principles. This treatment tells us that the principles are indeed held as true by all societies (i.e., they are universal in that sense), but that they also are held in a way that does not allow for exceptions (i.e., they are universal in a different sense). So 'do not kill others' is taken as being ambiguous, and in need of clarification. What it really is telling us is 'don't ever, under any circumstances, kill others'. Many pacifists accept this rendering. In effect, their version of the do not kill principle tells us that all wars are immoral or, put differently, it tells us never to go to war.

An absolutist with respect to the do not kill principle may find that it contains more ambiguities. For them, 'others' may be ambiguous as well. It could mean, '(others) who belong to our tribe', '(other) human beings' or even '(other) animals (including chimps, elephants, whales, etc.).'

However absolutists render the do not kill principle, they face the difficult problem of conflict. Consider the following scenario in the medical field. A doctor has been educated to believe that his duty, as a doctor, is to do his best to preserve life. He reads this rule in absolute terms. But he also treats the principle 'do what you can to minimize the suffering of others' in absolute terms. It is here that he gets into trouble. He may not see the trouble right away since he might have managed to get through his career so far by applying the one principle (absolutely) on one occasion, and the other (absolutely) on another occasion. But late in his career, he runs across a situation where in applying the one principle he cannot apply the other. One of his dying cancer patients is suffering terribly. But, as he sees it, the only way to stop his patient's suffering is to euthanize him – that is, to go against his do not kill principle. If the doctor takes that route, he goes against his principle by creating an exception to it. He thus abandons the idea that the principle is absolute. But if he stays with his version of the do not kill principle by refusing to make an exception to it, he is forced to abandon the absolutist status of the principle that tells him to do whatever he can to alleviate suffering.

In short, it is not possible to give two (basic) principles absolute status. Sooner or later they will come into conflict, and then one of the principles must be overridden. We can give one principle absolute status, but the other cannot help but have exceptions to it and thus have lesser status in the overall ethical scheme of things.

The second way to treat the universal principles is to concede at the outset that none is absolute. Instead, they all have what has been called presumptive status.[3] The principles can still be thought of as powerful and so the presumption is that they will hold in most situations. But they are not so powerful that exceptions to them are out of the question. Sooner or later, a conflict will develop, and one or more of the principles will be overridden in favour of another. The difference between the presumptive treatment of these principles and the absolute treatment is that, for the former, a principle that overrides some principles in certain circumstances may itself be overridden in other circumstances. No principle stands alone above the others all the time.

EXCEPTIONS

The process of making exceptions to what are being called universal principles is not unique to ethical principles. Exceptions are found in practical areas of life such as cooking, shopping, doing surgery, running a business, etc. If there are principles and rules that help us run our lives, there will inevitably be times when one or more of these principles and rules will 'fail' us because of conflict.

It is important to be clear here. Exceptions *are* exceptional. Principles and rules would not have the status they have unless they work for us in most situations. A principle (or rule) with so many exceptions to it that it cannot properly be cited as a guide to our behaviour would no longer be a principle. It would be a pseudo principle or, perhaps, a former principle. Living principles and rules do their work day and night, week in week out, year after year. As a result, we eventually follow them more through habit than by deliberation. And since habits are hard to break, the business of making exceptions to our principles and rules – breaking our habits – is likely to be difficult.

Actually, we want it to be difficult. If our principles and rules have stood the test of time in guiding our behaviour, we should be reluctant to weaken them by making exceptions one after another. Caution is the order of the day here.

A natural way to express that caution is by not allowing for exceptions unless there are very good reasons for doing so.[4] In medicine the no harm principle is very important. If an exception is going to be made to it, doctors and their patients insist that there must be at least one good reason for doing so. Well, one good reason for harming a patient via surgery is that the patient is suffering from internal bleeding caused by a serious fissure in her bowels. In journalism, one good reason for telling a lie (e.g., by the journalist presenting herself as a medical doctor) is that the doctors at the local mental hospital are thought to be abusing their patients. With her lie, the journalist is attempting to gain access to see if the allegations are true. In law, the lawyer makes an exception to the confidentiality rule because he has a good reason for doing so such as that he knows his client is about to commit a monstrous crime. Similarly, good reasons, different in their specifics, are cited for making exceptions in education (with respect to confidentiality for example), in business (with respect to moving a factory from a small town that employs 300 people) and in family matters (when one is considering filing for divorce).

In all these realms of ethics, the exceptions will be granted reluctantly.[5] But the reluctance will vary from one realm to another, and in terms of the situation within a realm. In medicine, good reasons are needed to justify minor surgery, but these reasons need not be that good. In law, by contrast, the reasons need to be stronger when confidentiality is breached. Is the client really about to commit a major crime? Is the HIV-infected client having sex with all kinds of people and thus spreading a dangerous disease?

There may even be settings in which the reasons have to be stronger still. Consider one in which important medical research is being done.[6] The presumption is that the researchers will not fabricate or manipulate the data they are gathering. The truth telling rule is extremely strong here. It seems to apply to all imaginable research settings. Still, if we try hard enough, we can imagine settings that allow for exceptions. You and I are engaged in government research. In the middle of our project we discover that the government plans to use our research results to harm certain ethnic groups in society. Might we not feel justified in sabotaging the research both by destroying and fabricating data?

The lesson to be learned from considering how exceptions are made to important principles and rules is that the exceptions process does not vary very much as we move from one realm of ethics to another. All who are involved in the exceptions business will be looking for one kind of good reason or another. As is clear from the examples cited above, the actual good reasons will vary from realm to realm. The good reasons in medicine (we will lessen physical and mental suffering if we make an exception by helping our patient die) will be different from those in law (we will save a life if we break confidentiality). There will also be variations in the stringency of the principles and rules. Exceptions will be more common in some settings than others. But the basic idea of looking for good reasons when one is thinking of making exceptions to one's favourite principles and rules will still be there.

WAR

So far I have avoided discussing the realm of war. I have done that deliberately in order to lead into saying that in war there is nothing exceptional about making exceptions to the no killing principle and perhaps to other principles as well. Good reasons for making exceptions in war are going to be in place just as they are in medicine, journalism, law and other moral realms.

On thinking about war, however, one might expect one difference. It might be supposed that the exceptions process would be more stringent when compared with the other realms. The consequences of a journalist making an exception to the truth telling rule are often quite serious, but they are not literally earth-shaking. Even the consequences of a doctor euthanizing a single patient, as serious as that is, are not earth-shaking. But the consequences of going to war are. In war, hundreds, thousands and even millions of people may die; many more than that may be injured. If war represents exceptions to the no killing and the no harm principles, it does so on a massive scale. Thus, this initial look at war suggests that the good reasons for going to war are going to have to be very good indeed. More will be said about these good reasons in the next chapter.

For now however, it is important to understand that the process of finding exceptions to our moral principles and rules in any realm does not end when good reasons have been found.

Other steps need to be taken as well. One can appreciate why by thinking, once again, about a case in medicine. The surgeon decides that harming the patient via a surgical procedure is justified. The procedure will after all remove the tumour that is endangering the patient's life. So the doctor has a good reason for making an exception to the no harm principle. But before he takes his patient to the surgical room he will ask himself: is there a less harmful way to rid ourselves of this ugly tumour? Radiation might do it. Chemotherapy might do it. Or, maybe, some combination of radiation and chemotherapy would get the job done.

What the doctor is doing is considering what other options he has. The same sort of process guides the behaviour of our journalist who is thinking about making exceptions to the truth-telling rule. She may very well have good reasons for making an exception. But before she does, she needs to (or she should) ask herself whether she can achieve the good she seeks by some other means. If she can gather the information she needs by looking at public records, or in some other public way, then she need not make an exception by means of lying. The lawyer too must look to other options before he makes an exception to the confidentiality principle in order to keep his client from committing his monstrous crime. He might try to talk the bad guy out of doing what he is planning to do.

It is no different with war. Even if a nation has good reasons (whatever they might be) for going to war, that is not enough to justify fully sending the nation's military forces into battle. Since war is such an awful option, other means need to (or should) be explored first. So at least in many war-threatening situations, negotiations should be tried. Sanctions might be tried as well.

So like the other realms of ethics, two steps, rather than just one, need to be taken before a nation can be said to be justified in entering a war. There are actually more than two steps: there are several. One, for instance, can be (and is) called likelihood of success. This step tells us that we should not make an exception to an important moral principle even if we have good reasons for doing so – and even if we have explored other options – provided we are not likely to succeed in accomplishing anything. If the surgery is almost certainly going to kill the patient while she is still in the surgical room, there is no point in carrying it out. Or if the patient is likely to be dead in two weeks no matter what we do, performing surgery is again pointless. Similarly, if a nation is considering entering a hopeless war where it is totally outnumbered, then it should simply raise hands in surrender.

There are therefore steps in common no matter what realm we consider. This represents an important insight when it comes to understanding the role of ethics in war. That role could be understood in other ways. It could be understood as part of a historical tradition that gradually identified this and that step in the process of helping rulers and soldiers decide what to do when war is at their doorstep. Or the steps could be identified more straightforwardly by applying well-known ethical theories such as utilitarianism and Kantianism. More than likely each of these approaches can tell us something interesting about the ethics of war. Ethical theories are like that. Each major theory approaches ethics from a different direction and so each tells us something we might not have thought about. So the approach to ethics, more particularly the ethics of war, in this study tells us things we might not have thought of. Indeed, being a different approach from the well-known theories we all study in philosophy, it is more likely to tell us something new. So far, what it tells us is how the ethics of war is related to the ethics of medicine, law, business and all the other realms. All of them need to deal with exceptions to principles and rules, both universal and not universal, and they inevitably need to deal with them in near-identical ways.

In the next chapter, I begin the discussion of the ethics of war as an attempt to deal with exceptions to important ethical principles and rules in war. The particular focus of that chapter is a presentation of the theory of war ethics as it is held by most of those who think seriously about war and war ethics.

2 Just War Theory

INTRODUCTION

Humans have been worried about war's horrors since recorded history and, perhaps, before that. From the beginning, they raised questions about the ethics of war. Ancient Chinese thinkers such as Confucius,[1] Mencius,[2] Mo Tzu[3] and various Taoists wondered openly about how war's horrors could be curtailed. The ancient Greeks, Plato[4] and Aristotle[5] among others, as well as thinkers from India,[6] shared these concerns. But in many of their writings, these thinkers did not present us with full-blown theories about the ethics of war. Instead, they gave us building blocks that eventually developed into theories. These building blocks began to take shape as theories during the period in European history when Christianity took hold,[7] and in the Middle East and north Africa when Islam became dominant.[8] Eventually, beginning in the seventeenth century, some thinkers took off the religious mantle that had previously shrouded these theories.[9] In Europe at least, but not necessarily in the Islamic world, some of these theories became secular while other versions stayed sectarian. It has continued that way to this day.

It is appropriate at the outset to make three points about these theories. First, they collectively came to be known as Just War Theory (JWT).[10] This is the family name for a group of closely related and overlapping theories. Second, although these theories are derived from widely disparate traditions, it is remarkable how much alike they are. They seem to differ more in detail than in substance. Third, especially after the Peace of Westphalia (1648), these very similar theories were mostly conceived of as taking the interests of nations into account. If the overall aim of this or that version of JWT was to restrain war, a more specific aim was to restrain nations from going to war with one another. Another aim was to put restraints on nations once war started.

Because JWT is a family name for various theories about the ethics of war, it is possible to formulate a kind of generic version of the theory that represents the thinking of most of the family members. There follows such an account. It is a first approximation of JWT. Details and problems with the theory will emerge in later chapters. This first approximation account identifies what the main principles of JWT are, and gives some indication as to why these principles belong in the theory.

Traditionally, the first part of Just War Theory (JWT) addresses issues pertaining to the start of war. The formal name for this is justice of the war (*jus ad bellum*). Put in terms of the discussion in the previous chapter, this first part asks: is a nation justified in starting a war, and so justified in making exceptions to one or more major ethical principles? To test whether the nation is justified, the theory presents those who are contemplating going to war with six principles. These principles act as hurdles to be cleared before a nation can say that it has justice on its side when it enters a war.

PART 1 JUSTICE OF THE WAR (*JUS AD BELLUM*)

a. Just Cause

In the previous chapter the first principle or hurdle was called the good reasons principle. JWT calls it the just cause principle. As it is usually articulated, the principle does more than merely tell us that we must have good reasons – indeed very good ones – before entering a war. It identifies the good reasons in some detail. If, the principle says, one nation is presently being attacked by another, that represents a good reason for the victim nation to send its troops into battle. If the attack is over, but has taken place recently, that too represents a good reason or just cause. In 1982, when the Argentinians occupied what they called the Malvinas Islands (the Falklands), the British could not respond immediately, but in a matter of weeks they gathered enough ships, troops and airplanes to take back the islands in decisive fashion. So although their response was delayed, it was still justified.

These responses to aggression presumably count as good reasons, because they rest upon fundamental ethical principles of one sort or another. Briefly, one theorist might say that responding to aggression is justified because aggressors do great harm to victim nations, not just in the actual attack but in its aftermath.[11] Once a nation has been taken over by another, the prostrate country can be exploited, plundered and even totally obliterated. Fighting a war is itself a costly endeavour but – so the argument goes – not fighting and therefore submitting to the aggressor nation is (usually) more costly. So in terms of counting the costs of entering or not entering war, entering is less costly and therefore justified.

A somewhat different 'fundamental' theory leads to the same conclusion. This theory starts by placing a high value on human independence (i.e., autonomy).[12] Humans act as humans when they are allowed to express their autonomy (i.e., their will) in how they are to live. Aggression by another nation deprives the victims of their autonomy. Those who would lose their autonomy if the aggression is not resisted therefore have every right to protect their autonomy by going to war.

Still other fundamental theories (e.g., rights-based, virtue and religious theories) can present arguments to show that responding to aggression is justified. So there is no problem dealing with present and recent acts of aggression within JWT.

But Just War Theory allows for other good reasons for going to war (i.e., for still more exceptions to the no killing and other rules).

Some of these reasons are not very controversial. The theory tells us that if another country is invaded, not only that nation but its allies (acting as good neighbours would) are justified in going to war. As before, the invasion can be ongoing or recent. Either way, the justification for going to war is much the same as when the nation helping its ally is itself attacked.

There are traditionally two other good reasons found within JWT for going to war. The first of these is also not very controversial. The second is. The first deals with humanitarian intervention.[13] If a nation is conducting genocide or genocide-like activity against a large group of its own citizens or the citizens of a conquered nation, humanitarian intervention is justified. Such intervention is also justified if a nation's government is simply unable to govern effectively so that chaos results. At first glance, this form of intervention appears to be difficult to justify, because the intervening nations are starting a war: they look like aggressors. But they are not the original aggressors in those settings where the other nation is at war with some of its own people. As to those other settings where a government has lost control of its affairs so that chaos is everywhere, there is, technically, no war going on. Still, there is much suffering taking place amidst the chaos, so it is to the suffering caused to which the intervening nation is responding. One of many ways to justify this sort of intervention is to calculate that the costs (to the suffering people) of not intervening are much greater than the costs of triggering a war whose aim is to alleviate their suffering.

Those arguing from an autonomy theory would express the matter in their own special terms: they would say that the chaos is causing great losses of autonomy. Intervention would, they add, restore much of that autonomy.

The last major good reason that falls under the heading of the just cause principle is indeed controversial. Unlike the good reasons concerned with an attack in the present or in the recent past, this one is concerned with the immediate future. It tells us that if a nation has extremely strong evidence that an attack by a potential enemy is serious and imminent, a preemptive strike is permitted.[14] It is not clear what time-scale would count as imminent. But certainly if preparations such as fuelling airplanes, loading them with munitions and moving major ground forces armed and ready for attack towards the border are being made, those on the other side of the border have reason for concern. Further, if their concern is augmented by intelligence telling them that they will be attacked, then a preemptive strike is justified.

What is not clear is just how far into the future the threat can be. What if the attack is scheduled to begin a week from today? What about one scheduled a month from now? At some point if an attack is initiated, it becomes preventive rather than preemptive. A preventive strike is one designed to stop an expected enemy attack in the distant future – one, two, five years from now. As will be made clear immediately below, JWT does not permit preventive strikes. But it does permit preemptive ones, especially if the imminence of the attack is a matter of hours.[15]

There are, then, six specific good reasons that give content to the just cause principle. Three are related to self-defence, and three to the defence of others.

Just Cause

Defence of own nation	*Defence of others*
when under attack	when under attack
when under recent attack	when under recent attack
when about to be attacked	when genocide is taking place or when a nation is in chaos

Perhaps one final point about just cause needs to be made. Although they rarely make it explicit, many just war theorists suppose that the list, or one just like it, is exhaustive. For them, there are six just cause sub-principles, and that is all. To put it differently, they assume that there are no other good reasons for going to war. They resist the suggestion that it is possible to extend the list since that would make it easier for nations to make war. The job of JWT is to restrain war, so every effort should be made to keep the good reasons list for war down to a minimum.

In Chapter 6, I will examine this assumption and then go on to argue that it should be abandoned. The argument will be that the assumption makes JWT so rigid that it cannot deal with the variety of situations that prompt humans to go to war with one another.

b. Last Resort

The last resort principle helps explain why Just War Theory does not allow preventive wars. Since the threat of war prompting a preventive response is in the distant future, there is time to take steps to avoid it. Negotiations can be tried; so can boycotts, sanctions and deadlines. These and other steps short of war can be tried in different combinations.

What the last resort principle tells us is that these steps should be tried first because wars represent the worst option open to leaders who are walking (stumbling?) in the direction of war. As the worst option, war should be tried last.

Unfortunately, in one important respect, the last resort principle is an example of hyperbole. A nation cannot choose war as a last resort since, taken literally, 'last resort' is meaningless. There simply is no way to identify war as last after *all* the others have been tried. Some dignitary can always point to something else that can be done to avoid war even if a dozen or so efforts towards that end have already been tried. And when another dignitary suggests another resort short of war after the first dignitary's effort has failed, it becomes obvious that we have an infinite regress on our hands.

So if last resort is to have meaning, it must mean something other than what it says it means. It must mean that nations should not enter war until war is the last *reasonable* resort.[16] What 'reasonable' means is rarely made clear: it is a terribly vague concept. But minimally it means this much. Since war is taken by just war theorists to be the most harmful option, it should never be undertaken 'at the drop of a hat'. Instead, at least several options short of war should be tried before a nation starts shooting.

One other point about last resort needs to be made in this initial look at the last resort principle. The principle has limited application in situations where a nation or one of its allies is already under attack. It makes little sense to talk of negotiating, trying sanctions and the like when the other side is already moving its troops across the border. There is still the decision to be made about resisting the aggression or not. But aside from that, last resort has no application. The principle is moot in these situations.

c and d. Proportionality and Likelihood of Success

These two principles are close enough in meaning to be easily confused with one another.[17] Proportionality is concerned with estimates of costs and benefits of a war if it is successful. What the principle demands is that the estimates of benefit be (significantly?) greater than the cost. War, of course, is full of imponderables so that these estimates are at best rough and ready. But the principle demands that estimates be made anyway. When they are, and when these estimates show that the costs are projected to be far greater than the benefits, the principle tells us that a war should not be undertaken. In most other situations, as when the estimated benefits are slightly greater than the costs, the principle is either silent or it tells us that war is permissible.

Whereas the proportionality principle is used to estimate the good and bad of a possible war if it is successful, the likelihood of success principle estimates how successful the war itself will be.[18] As with proportionality, it is not always clear at what point the likelihood of success principle forbids war. It does so clearly when the situation is hopeless. In World War II it did not recommend that Luxembourg resist the Wehrmacht as it passed through that small nation on its way to France. Yet even if the situation is dire, as it was with Belgium in that same war, the principle does not necessarily forbid war.

Part of the problem with the principle lies in the meaning of the word 'success'. In one situation it may mean the total destruction of enemy forces. In another it may mean holding the enemy at bay. In still another it may mean making the enemy pay dearly for whatever gains it makes. It may even mean survival. In the 2006 war with Israel, some Hezbollah officials claimed that they were successful because they and some members of their organization survived the war.

Then there is the related problem that those who assess what 'success' means speak ambiguously. At the beginning of war, when the rhetoric of war is at its height, nothing less than total victory is demanded and promised. But once reality sets in and it becomes obvious that total victory is unachievable, some lesser sense of success becomes the accepted standard.

In spite of these problems with the success principle, and with those found in the proportionality principle, both principles can still be applied often enough to retain their status within Just War Theory. How important their status is will become evident as the discussion develops in later chapters.

e. Right Intentions

The four principles within Just War Theory discussed thus far are all procedural in nature. They tell those who are making decisions about war how to go about making those decisions: they should look for good reasons, look to war as an option only after other options have been explored, look for the benefits of war to be greater than the costs and look for some likelihood that the war effort will be successful. The right intentions principle apparently does not add any new procedural insights. It does not tell us what else to do by way of figuring out whether to go to war or not. Instead, it enquires into the mental state of those who are making the war-or-no-war decision.

So what mental state should those who are making war decisions be in? Certainly not the mental state of an aggressor.[19] An aggressor nation acts for selfish gain and, in so doing, is usually willing to harm others. Certainly also not in the mental state of an exploiter. When a nation enters a war ostensibly to rescue another nation from occupation but then, once the rescue is over, engages in exploitation, it is taking advantage of the situation. In the end it harms the people it has saved. Aggressors and exploiters have bad intentions.

But then what are good or right intentions? To answer this question a distinction between motivation and intentions needs to be made. The former has to do with the drive or energy that leads to some action, the latter with what actions are triggered by the motivation. It is thus a mistake to say that a nation or some military personnel have the wrong intentions when they go to war with hate in their heart, or they have the right intentions when they love their enemy. Hate and love are forms of motivation, not kinds of intentions. Intentions speak to actions. Having the right intention, then, is more like aiming to act in accordance with just cause. If the just cause is that an aggressor has invaded our neighbours' territory, then having the right intention means doing what can be done to stop the invasion. Another example of having the right intention would be when a nation takes steps to liberate a friendly nation that has been recently occupied. Still another example would be when a nation takes steps to stop a humanitarian disaster. In all these cases of having the right intentions, the nation involved does its good work and then retires its military forces from the scene so that the saved, liberated, or the disaster-prone nation is allowed to resume its affairs without excessive interference from the nation that has helped it.

One of the peculiarities of right intentions is that assessment of intentions by others can only be done (effectively) after the fact. When they enter a war, all nations claim that they have right intentions. To be sure, in some cases it will be patently clear that the claims are false. Germany's claim in 1939 that Poland started the war, and that Germany's intention was to stop an aggressor, fooled no one. But in many cases the situation is so complicated that it is impossible to tell at the start what the real intentions of a nation entering a war are. It may later all become clear. If, for example, the liberating army stays on well after the war is over, and stays on against the will of the country it has liberated, it becomes obvious that that nation's intentions were not good.

f. Legitimate Authority

Like right intentions, this is not a process principle. It does not purport to identify a step in the process of deciding whether or not to enter a war. Rather it identifies those who have been given the power to engage in the decisionmaking process.[20] That power might reside in a king, a chancellor, a dictator, a council, or a legislative body. The locus of authority varies with the nation. If the legitimate authority sanctions a war, one step in going to war legally has been satisfied. If, however, the war is authorized by some individual or group other than the legitimate authority, then the war is automatically unjust. Of course, some local warlord might actually trigger a war by sending his faithful followers across the border on a mission of violence.[21] But such a war, although real and possibly devastating, would be unjust.

Unlike the right intentions with its subjective character, legitimate authority is objective because it is a public principle. The authority is identified by laws of the state that are clear to everyone who should know about them. So, historically, at least up to and a few years beyond World War II, there was not much controversy about whether this war or that war was properly authorized. Controversy has arisen, however, with the advent of the United Nations. Some say that the UN is now the legitimate authority, especially with respect to humanitarian wars. Others take the stance that although the UN has some authority, that authority does not override the power of the nation state.

This has been a preliminary look at part 1 (justice of the war) of Just War Theory. Six principles have been identified as forming this part of the theory. According to the usual interpretation of the theory, all the principles need to be satisfied. A failure to meet the standard set by any one of them leads to a judgement that the war is unjust. Apparently – although this is not totally clear – there are no degrees of injustice. It is not as if when some principles are not satisfied one commits a greater injustice while when others are not satisfied some lesser form of injustice is committed. It appears that an injustice is an injustice, and that is the end of the matter.

Here, in summary form, are the six justice of the war (*jus ad bellum*) principles.

Just Cause

Imminent, present and recent acts of aggression (against one's own country or an 'ally') count as good reasons for going to war. So do humanitarian catastrophes.

Last Resort

This principle slows down the process of going to war by asking the potential participants to make a series of efforts to avoid war. The intention of the principle is to retard the process of going to war so that, in some cases, war never breaks out.

Proportionality

This is a benefits versus costs principle. Overall, it tells us that since war is such a horrible way to settle disputes, the potential participants to a war should estimate that, if successful, the benefits definitely outweigh the costs of going to war.

Likelihood of Success

This principle advises that a war should not be entered into if there is little or no chance that it will meet with some degree of success.

Right Intentions

Intentions should not be confused with motives. What is required is not that one's motives be pure or mostly good, but that the intentions to do something are right. Right intentions are more often than not tied to just cause. If a nation intends to act in order to correct an injustice, and does not act additionally in ways that lead to its own aggression or to exploitation, then it can be said to have right intentions.

Legitimate Authority

This is a public principle. It says that only those who are legally designated to make decisions about going or not going to war be permitted to do so. All others, if they trigger war by their actions, are acting unjustly.

PART 2 JUSTICE IN THE WAR (*JUS IN BELLO*)

Part 1 of Just War Theory is the part shared by other theories of ethics that reside in domains such as medicine, business, journalism and law. All of these theories are concerned with making exceptions to principles and rules when they do their work, and all need principles like the ones developed in JWT to get that job done. However, war demands something more, because it is a state of affairs not an event or occurrence. When a doctor considers surgery as a way of treating his patient's disorder he is concerned about an event that would take place over a short period of time. The surgery and the brief follow-up medical care might take six hours or so and a couple of weeks respectively. What the doctor does in cutting into his patient can be justified or not within the framework of medicine's version of Part 1. So for medicine and most of the other domains that might develop an exceptions theory, all that is needed is Part 1.

But war is different in referring to a state, not an occurrence or event. We speak of being in a state of war. What this means is that war lasts for weeks, months or years. This being so, it is easy to separate that part of a theory of exceptions having to do with starting a war (justice of the war) and the protracted period of time that follows once the war is started (justice in the war). Put differently, because war is long-lasting, many things can happen once it starts that cannot possibly be covered by that part of the theory concerned with starting or not starting the war. So Part 2 tells the war participants how they can fight the war while maintaining a sense of justice (ethics). According to the theory, they can do this by following two principles:

a. Proportionality

Proportionality in the justice of the war (*jus ad bellum*) portion of JWT is concerned with the whole of a war. Now in the justice in the war portion, proportionality is concerned with individual battles and/or campaigns.[22] The principle distinguishes between applying excessive and overwhelming force. Excessive force does more damage (both to the enemy and to 'our side') in battle than is necessary. One applies excessive force, for example, in mounting a major attack on a fortress that, in fact, is about to surrender. In such a situation, lives on both sides are wasted. Here is another example of excessive force. A sniper fires from the top of a hill; there are both soldiers and civilians at or near that hill. Fighter bombers are ordered to the scene and they promptly kill everyone there by obliterating the hill. Here is still another example. A general wishes to gain glory by being the one to capture the enemy capital city. He is in competition with fellow generals to get the job done. To get the glory, he incurs very heavy casualties among his own troops and also causes heavy casualties among enemy civilians. Had he not been in such a rush to occupy the capital, many lives would have been spared on both sides.

Whereas the proportionality principle condemns use of excessive force, it does not necessarily condemn using overwhelming force. Using overwhelming force may actually save lives. Instead of attacking an enemy in piecemeal fashion, a bold and powerful attack may induce the enemy not to yield serious resistance. As a result, the enemy loses the fight but does not lose many lives. Likewise, the attacking side's casualties are less than they otherwise might be.

Whether the attack is overwhelming or not, the principle gives advice to commanders as follows:

1. Identify the options available to the attacking (or even the defending) force and choose the option that is projected to cause the least excessive damage.
2. Once the best option is identified, if it proves that that option will in all likelihood also cause excessive damage, desist from attacking the target (or defending whatever land one is holding).

The justice-in-the-war version of proportionality suffers from the same defect as does the justice-of-the-war version. Both versions have a measurement problem. Given the fog of war, there are difficulties in calculating the benefits and costs in advance of the war in the one case, and in advance of the battle in the other. About all one can hope to do is identify wars and battles that will have obvious conclusions and so make it possible to determine that this war or that battle will cause disproportionate damage.

b. Discrimination

The principle of discrimination is, perhaps along with just cause, the most important principle in Just War Theory.[23] It demands that those who participate in war should distinguish between legitimate targets and non-legitimate targets. Permitted targets include members of a military establishment, those who provide the military with equipment and supplies and those civilians who work directly or lead the military; but those who work as and for civilians – mothers, children, retired people, religious leaders and medical personnel – are not legitimate targets. Similarly, military facilities, military factories and trains bringing supplies to the front are subject to attack; but civilian factories, religious institutions, hospitals, schools and the like are not.

Everyone understands that it is not always easy to draw a line between what should and should not be attacked. Should a bridge, for instance, that is used mostly by civilians to take food to market but is also used by the military 'on a priority basis' be attacked? What about a factory that produces clothing both for civilians and military personnel? What if the production is 50–50? What if, to complicate matters, the factory is operated 24 hours a day, seven days a week? Does the principle give guidance on whether it can be attacked? In short, the principle has some vagueness to it. It is not always clear where the line between 'those who can be attacked' and 'those who cannot' is to be drawn. Still, in the vast majority of situations that military personnel find themselves facing, the line is clear enough so that the principle can be applied more often than not. It is because it has wide application that it can be thought of as an important principle in Just War Theory.

Like just cause and some of the other principles, justifying the discrimination principle is not difficult. It can be done in terms of autonomy by noting that indiscriminate war takes away the autonomy of more people than does a war that discriminates. Or it can be justified in terms of rights. Indiscriminate war violates rights of people far beyond what is required to pursue victory in war. It can even be justified in consequential, more particularly utilitarian, terms. Under such a theory it can be argued that indiscriminate war harms more people on both sides than is necessary to prevail in war. Because the principle can be justified in more ways than one, how it is justified does not appear to be an important consideration. What seems important is that the principle itself is in place in the theory.

FINAL PRELIMINARY COMMENTS

As noted already, the above version of Just War Theory does not have any sort of official status. Rather, it is a composite version of a theory that has gone through many iterations over time.

A version of JWT has been presented here in order to serve as a starting or reference point for later examining the theory in greater detail. Of the many questions that will be asked about the theory, the most important is the following: does the theory need to be modified in order to make it possible to deal with modern war? War has changed significantly since the two world wars. Technology alone has transformed war so that the enemy can be attacked almost instantly anywhere in the world, day or night, in good weather or foul, and with powerful smart weapons. Do any or any combination of these changes mean, for instance, that the principle of discrimination has to be modified?

But wars have changed in another way, and that change also raises questions about whether JWT needs to be modified. Politics has changed. No longer do conflicts take place mainly between two nations. Today wars between nations on the one side and non-nation groups on the other dominate our attention. Do these political changes warrant making changes in JWT? These, and other related questions, will be dealt with in the chapters that follow.

3 Objections to Just War Theory

FOUR OBJECTIONS

Enough has already been said about Just War Theory to make it clear that it has detractors as well as supporters. If nothing else, the very complexity of the theory makes it an inviting target for criticism. If one part of the theory can't be attacked, the thinking goes, surely another part can be. Not surprisingly, then, one does not have long to wait for the attacks to start.

Perhaps the most common of these attacks is simply that nations do not employ the theory very often or at all. Nations, it is said, go to war for selfish, not ethical, reasons. The reason nations give most often when they want to go to war is 'it is in our interest to do so' or 'we need to act to protect our interests'. On the other side, those not in favour of entering a war express themselves by asking such rhetorical questions as 'what interests do we have here?' Both sides, then, tend to frame the discussion about entering war in terms of interests. It is as if for them ethical concerns, as expressed in JWT, are irrelevant to the discussion.

Another common criticism is closely tied to the first. It goes something like this. Nations do sometimes use JWT. It is not as if they are unaware of the theory's existence. But they use it as window dressing. It makes good public relations to invoke ethical concerns such as those found in JWT. They say things such as 'we are not aggressors, the enemy is' and 'we have sent in our troops for humanitarian reasons'. Those who use these expressions pretend that they are acting in accordance with ethical standards but, when the chips are down, become involved in war or not from self-interest.

A third criticism is an extension of the second. This criticism notes that even when rulers in charge of making decisions about war seriously invoke the theory, they find it to be extremely plastic or 'loose'. If they are inclined to go to war, they find that its principles can be moulded in such a way as to allow them to satisfy their inclinations. So these governmental officials are not just using JWT as window dressing. Nor are they necessarily being cynical in invoking the theory: they may sincerely believe that they are following its principles. They may even sincerely believe that they are not walking down the path of self-interest. But they are. Their thinking is simply confused.

This third criticism can, with a twist, be used by those who profess to be pacifists. Pacifists, of course, are not sympathetic to JWT. Followers of JWT tell us that some wars can be justified, while others cannot be. Supposedly, then, they use their theory to distinguish between justified and unjustified wars. Pacifists, in contrast, argue that no wars are justified,[1] so in a sense have no use for JWT. Yet in another sense they can use the theory because of its plasticity. They can pretend, somewhat cynically, that they are just war theorists. They might publicly concede that it is possible to justify certain wars even as they make it clear that they believe that most wars cannot be justified. But when they apply the JWT principles, they do so in such a strict manner that no wars are in fact justified. For example, they say that when they employ the proportionality principle they find that this war, that one and that one too is each more costly than abject surrender. They also emphasize the point made in the previous chapter about last resort. We must, they say, make another effort before we go to war. And when that effort fails, they argue for still another effort. Even when last resort is interpreted to mean last reasonable resort, they argue that there are still some reasonable resorts that have not yet been explored.

So the plastic or loose feature of JWT can be used both by those who want to wage war and by those who want to forbid it. That seems to show, when one steps back and looks at what both the war advocates and the pacifists say, that JWT is simply 'no damned good'.

A fourth criticism is also often heard. It comes from those who call themselves realists.[2] They do not deny that some governments, some of the time, follow the precepts of ethics in their relations with other governments. But they say that this is unfortunate. Those who work within the realm of ethics tend to be idealistic, utopian, legalistic, etc. That being so, they inevitably do more harm than good, because they focus too much on the ideal end result of their thinking instead of the means necessary to bring the end result about. These people are, in short, unrealistic: do-gooders who do not actually bring about good. In fact, they often do more harm than good.

WHO COULD USE JUST WAR THEORY? AND WHEN?

There is no quick and effective way of dealing with these four objections. The third objection (concerning JWT's plasticity or looseness) is especially difficult. Only after much more has been said about JWT can a plausible reply to this criticism be offered (in Chapter 11). Similarly, the fourth objection requires more discussion of JWT before it can be dealt with adequately. The same is true of the second objection. But the first one ('nobody uses the theory') is perhaps somewhat easier to deal with even if replying to it requires a bit of effort. The first step in that effort is to raise the following question: who could possibly use Just War Theory?

With regard to the justice of the war portion, the most obvious answer is those officials who are in charge of decisions about going to war. For many, this is not only the most obvious answer but the only one that really counts. They treat the justice of the war portion of JWT as the special preserve of these select officials. These officials are the ones in charge of war matters so they are the ones who must (or should) employ the theory. The purpose of the theory is to guide them. So if they fail to use it, the theory as a practical instrument for making decisions about war is nullified.

This argument about not using JWT makes some sense when dealing with dictatorships. When a typical dictator and his close associates make decisions about war, they probably give ethical considerations only scant attention at best. But democratic regimes are different. Although the final authority for going to war may well reside formally in one person, the war discussion is inevitably wide-ranging. Government officials not in the direct line of making decisions about war will have their say; so will individuals and groups in the mass media, academia, the churches and the general population.[3] Not all members of these groups will, in fact, speak out, but many will.

Of those who do speak out, they are not necessarily going to do so in accordance with any outlook that resembles JWT. Some will argue from a realist (i.e., self-interest) perspective while perhaps a smaller number from a pacifist perspective. But if the recent past is any indication, many will argue from the perspective of JWT. During the Gulf War of 1991, for example, those in America who favoured of liberating Kuwait trumpeted the principle of just cause. 'This (aggression)', President George H. W. Bush said, 'will not stand'. There was also much talk about last resort. Those on Bush's side argued that the coalition of nations prepared to go to war had reached the point of last reasonable resort. So they argued that it was in accord with JWT to go to war when the last deadline for acceding to UN demands was not met by the Iraqis.

Interestingly enough, in that same war, opponents to the invasion appealed to last resort as well. They argued that the coalition had not reached the point of last resort. They recognized that the principle of just cause could be cited to begin a war, but they focused on the last resort principle because they were opposed to starting the war in early 1991. Colin Powell, then secretary of defense, argued that sanctions should be tried for a year or two before the troops were sent into the field.[4] Sam Nunn, one of the senators from the state of Georgia, argued along the same lines.[5] They and others simply differed from the president's supporters in their interpretation of the last resort principle. The point is that the two sides did not differ in appealing to JWT. Both agreed that the debate should have taken place, and did, within the realm of JWT and not some theory based on self-interest.

The same general point can be made with respect to the war in Afghanistan and the 2003 Iraq War. The former war was less debated because it seemed clear to almost everyone that the coalition headed by the Americans had just cause to attack the Taliban regime and the al Qaeda forces that the Taliban was protecting. The latter war was more controversial, so the debates were endless. Still, in both, the various participants framed their arguments largely in terms of JWT.

Recall that the first argument against JWT was that it was not in fact used. Leaders in charge of making decisions about war, the claim was, think mainly in terms of self-interest (of the nation each one represents) rather than ethics. This claim has some plausibility, since much of the discussion by the leaders' inner circle takes place in secrecy and we just don't know what these power brokers are saying to one another. Very likely, even if there is some discussion of ethics, it is mixed with discussion of self-interest. One power broker would emphasize ethical considerations, while another self-interested ones, or even for ethics (and JWT) at one moment, and self-interest at another. We can't assume that power brokers are paragons of consistency.

Still, in a democratic society, many who are not a part of the inner circle argue publicly in terms of JWT and, directly or indirectly, pressure the power brokers into thinking in those terms as well. The outsiders who pressure the inner circle do not even have to be members of the nation making decisions about war – International pressure can work as well.

Seeing how JWT might be, and often is, used broadly by many individuals and groups lessens the tendency to believe that few use the theory to help them think through issues pertaining to the start of war. It still isn't clear just how much JWT thinking takes place when war is in the air. This is especially so since such thinking is often mixed in with self-interest thinking. But again, when one considers all the different groups that get into the act of deliberating about war, more thinking about JWT evidently takes place than might at first be supposed.

Looking at *when* JWT is employed, as opposed to *who* employs it, helps support this last point. It might be supposed that the ideal time to employ JWT is before the start of war. Such prospective use naturally comes to mind more than does retrospective use simply because we think that JWT should prevent war if it is to be good for anything. But the latter use is certainly quite common and important. Historians, political scientists, political commentators, ethicists, journalists, etc., spend much time raking over what happened. Some recent examples come to mind. Think of all the discussions about JWT during the Vietnam War, the Afghan-Russian war of the 1980s, the Falklands War of 1982, the Gulf War of 1991, the Chechen War in the 1990s, the Afghan War following 9/11 and the Iraq War of 2003. Perhaps because such retrospective use of JWT is so public, and because it is apparently never ending, the theory is probably used more retrospectively than prospectively.

USE OF JUST WAR THEORY – IN THE WAR

So far the discussion as to whether JWT is actually used by rulers and others has been concerned with justice of the war. And, so far, the conclusion is that it may have greater use than might at first be supposed. But, now, what of the use of the justice in the war portion of the theory? Is it being used these days in a robust manner? The answer is, apparently, yes. One does not have far to look to understand one major reason for this answer. Think for a moment what effect television has had on war, especially when it is broadcast globally by communication satellites. Today, if soldiers violate the principle of discrimination by committing atrocities against the civilian population, their deeds are not so easy to hide. Recall an incident during the Gulf War of 1991 where American F-117s bombed the Al Firdos bunker in the Ameriyya suburb of Baghdad because they thought it was a communications centre.[6] Evidently it was such a centre; but during the night it was also a place of refuge for civilians. Hundreds were killed. The very next day the Iraqi press touted the incident as an atrocity – a deliberate act that violated the discrimination principle. Reporters were given access to the damage and the carnage perpetrated by the F-117s. The whole world quickly knew what had happened. It later became evident that the killings were not intentional, but if they had been, television reporters would quickly have identified the culprits and blamed them by means of the discrimination principle.

The bombing of the bunker shows the principle of discrimination at work in another way. In bombing Baghdad during the 1991 war, the US Air Force used only 'state of the art' weaponry. The stealthy F-117s were conjoined with smart weaponry to enable these bombers both to hit their targets with hitherto unachievable accuracy and to avoid hitting civilian targets. Since that time, smart weaponry has become significantly smarter. Such weaponry has become the standard when it comes to targeting an enemy. The United States, and now other countries, spends billions of dollars in honouring the principle of discrimination.

There are more recent examples of how bad behaviour comes to haunt a modern military establishment. For example, it didn't take long for the mass media to uncover the abuses at Abu Ghraib prison.[7] It took a little longer but the events in Haditha late in 2005 came out early in 2006.[8] But they did come out. The tragic events in Lebanon and Israel in 2006 did not require time at all to become known. The mass media reported the hardships and loss of civilian life almost in real time and in most vivid terms.[9]

WHAT HASN'T BEEN SHOWN

The argument in this chapter is that Just War Theory is not an ignored creation of thinkers from the past. Initially it seems as if it has been and is being ignored. If one focuses heavily on the actions of those political leaders who have in their hands the power to start or not start wars, it is not clear what role JWT has to play in their thinking. If anything, self-interest thinking seems to dominate. However, if one looks more broadly at all sorts of individuals and groups who are concerned with the destructive power of war, it appears that JWT plays a significant role in their thinking and is thus not extinct.

I say 'appears' because there is room for doubt for the following reason. Principles such as last resort are not the exclusive preserve of JWT; this became clear in the discussion of the various domains of ethics in Chapter 1. Just medical theory appeals to that principle, or one much like it, when doctors think about surgery. They engage in such surgery only as a last resort. Similarly journalists make exceptions to their truth-telling principle only as a last resort. However, last resort can be appealed to by theorists who are concerned about war but are opposed to JWT. Realists can do so by arguing as follows. 'We too, like just war theorists, think that war is a most serious matter. War ought to be avoided as much as possible – for self-interest reasons. So we too choose war as a last resort – again for the sake of self-interest rather than for ethical reasons'.

The problem this sort of argument poses for the main thesis of this chapter is that when thinkers appeal to last resort, it is tempting to assume that they are working within the framework of JWT. The temptation to make this assumption increases when those who appeal to last resort do not present their whole position – they do not necessarily expand on their thinking and thereby explain why they are following the last resort principle. They may not even cite other principles that might show them to be just war or self-interest thinkers.

It may, therefore, turn out that some last resort thinking is not part of JWT. The same point can be made with regard to appeals to proportionality. Self-interest theorists can appeal to that principle as can just war theorists. They can argue that they will not go to war unless they feel that the gains of going to war will likely exceed the losses. So, again, if a thinker appeals to the principle of proportionality, one cannot automatically assume that the appeal is made within the framework of JWT.

Even if thinkers appeal to just cause, that may not be enough to brand them as followers of JWT. More than likely, they would call their just cause principle the good reasons principle. But it would resemble JWT's version by including a sub-principle that marks aggression against 'us' or our friends as a good reason for going to war. To be sure, it would differ in some respects since, for one, a self-interest theory would probably not have much to say about humanitarian intervention. Still, self-interest theories resemble JWT with regard to such principles as just cause, last resort, proportionality and perhaps some of the other principles so as to make it difficult to determine which theory an individual or a group is appealing to in order to answer questions about whether and how war is to be fought.

So I take it that, as of the end of this chapter, I have not shown clearly that JWT has been used extensively. Indeed, over time, it seems to have been used only sporadically. All I have done is merely to suggest that JWT *can* be used in various war settings. To show that JWT can have wide use, an examination of various wars is needed.

Further, in this chapter, I have said nothing about the window dressing criticism of that theory. Nor have I said anything about the criticism that JWT is loose or plastic so that it cannot give anyone meaningful guidance about war. Finally, I have said nothing about the claim that JWT and other moralistic outlooks are counterproductive (objection no. four). The next chapter begins the process of dealing with these issues. It does so with the help of a series of historical examples.

4 Easy Cases: Germany, Japan, Korea

THE GERMAN/POLISH WAR OF 1939

Applying Just War Theory retrospectively is never easy. There are always special circumstances in war that make for a bad fit for one or another of the theory's principles. Still, there are literally thousands of wars where, overall, the theory fits fairly well. In this chapter we look at a few such wars in beginning to deal with several of the objections raised in the previous chapter, but most particularly to deal with the claim that the theory is so loose that few if any conclusions can be drawn from it.

More often than not, a nation has its ways of justifying acts of aggression. In the minds of the leaders, it has good reasons (just cause) for what it is about to do. One such reason is to restore lands taken away in past wars. Another is that some of its own people living abroad are being oppressed. Still another is that the victim nation of the aggression is not really a victim since it is guilty of border incursions and other incidents. In 1939, Germany used all these reasons to justify its attack on Poland.

As it turned out, some of these reasons were exaggerations, while at least one was a fabrication. With respect to the latter, the Germans dressed political prisoners in Polish uniforms, executed them and then claimed that they had just repelled an attack by the Poles.[1] The Poles, they said, were the aggressors. No one was fooled except perhaps some true believers in Berlin. After all, it was Germany, not Poland, that had its military machine fully poised for a swift invasion of its neighbour. Also, as became clear later, it was Germany that had, several days prior to the invasion, signed a non-aggression pact with the USSR that included an agreement as to how Poland was to be divided once war started.[2] Further, Hitler had made it clear to some of his associates that the invasion of Poland was only an early step in the process of gaining sway over most of Europe.[3] So there was no doubt who the aggressor was. None of the reasons that Germany gave for invading Poland rose to the level of satisfying just cause.

Poland, of course, had just cause for fighting. She was fighting a defensive war against Germany and, soon enough, against the USSR. As it turned out, the odds that she could succeed in her effort to protect herself were prohibitively high. It might seem, therefore, that she could not satisfy the likelihood of success principle. But *prior* to the war, very few either in Poland or elsewhere had any realistic sense about what the odds were. The concept of *blitzkrieg* was as yet unknown. It was evident that Germany's military might was growing, but it still made sense to suppose that, with help from the French who were expected to launch an offensive (but didn't) in the west, Poland could put up a good fight. So Poland satisfied the success principle. It also satisfied the proportionality principle. If she were successful, the good of fighting for her independence should outweigh the costs in lives of resisting the Germans and in living under an oppressor's heel. As to last resort, that principle was moot: the war had started so Poland had no resorts prior to war to which to appeal. Poland also satisfied the other principles in the theory. Her intentions were good insofar as they were aimed at stopping German aggression and nothing else. There was, finally, no problem with the legitimate authority principle; the Polish army, air force and navy were all fighting with the approval of the legitimate government of Poland.

As to Germany, she not only violated the just cause principle but also the last resort principle. In the negotiations prior to the war, Hitler made unreasonable demands on Poland. In effect, what he asked for would have turned Poland into a German 'satellite'.[4] Had the Poles acceded to Hitler's demands, they would have practically negotiated themselves out of existence. It is clear then that Hitler was not negotiating in good faith, but no matter, he cut short the negotiations when he deemed that it was time to go to war.

Hitler, more or less, was in accord with two of the other principles of the *jus ad bellum* portion of Just War Theory: he was the proper authority to call for war and he had a good likelihood of success. There is a problem, however, with the proportionality principle. If Hitler had applied the principle, he probably would have done so in such a manner as to show more benefit than harm to *Germany*. And he probably made such an assessment. But the proportionality principle is not restrictive by way of favouring one group over another. Its proper application takes into account the interests of everyone involved in a war. Had Hitler made an assessment that took account not only of benefits and costs to Germans but also to the Poles, his invasion could not have satisfied the principle. But, in a way, all that is irrelevant. As already noted, the Germans failed to satisfy the just cause and the last resort principles, and that is enough to warrant making the judgement that the war against Poland was unjust. No doubt, Hitler violated one other principle: in threatening the Poles, he could not possibly have satisfied the good intentions principle. One might say that his actions and plans had bad, not good, intentions built into them.

The Germans acted unjustly as well with respect to at least one of the *in bello* principles of Just War Theory: the principle of discrimination. The Germans probably did not seriously violate that principle at the beginning of the war; they were too busy fighting the Polish military to have time to misbehave. But soon enough, even before the war was over, Warsaw was bombed in such a way that there were high civilian casualties. Also, soon enough, the SS got into position so it could do much harm to large segments of the Polish population.

It is not clear whether the Germans violated the (*in bello*) proportionality principle. They seemed to have deployed and used their forces against the Poles in accordance with standard military practices. They did not seem to have gone out of their way to cause excessive harm in the battles as such. That they mistreated their prisoners after the war was over is another matter. Mistreating prisoners however, is usually taken as a violation of the discrimination principle, since prisoners are no longer thought of as engaged in any kind of war activity.

In the end, then, even if the Germans are given the benefit of the doubt with respect to proportionality, it is clear that they thoroughly violated a total of three just war principles (just cause, last resort and discrimination); and that is enough to warrant condemning them.

SOME OTHER GERMAN CAMPAIGNS IN WORLD WAR II

In many respects, Barbarossa, the German campaign in 1941 against the USSR, is similar to the Polish campaign. The attacks were unprovoked, unannounced and ruthless, and so violated the same principles of Just War Theory as those violated in Poland. But before Hitler could launch Barbarossa, he wanted to secure his right flank. He did not want to advance into Russia and thereby give the British an opportunity to attack him from behind through the Balkans.[5] So he and his powerful military machine targeted Greece. Yugoslavia was drawn in to cooperate with the Germans in this endeavour by joining the Axis powers and giving the German army access to Greece. But a coup changed all that. The new Yugoslav government would not cooperate with the Germans, so Yugoslavia had to be invaded as well.[6] It is clear that the attacks on Yugoslavia and Greece were acts of aggression. There was no just cause at play here at all. In no sense of the word could the Germans claim that they fought these nations for defensive reasons, for reasons of preemption, or for humanitarian reasons. They attacked so that Hitler could support another act of aggression. To make matters worse, the attacks clearly also violated the last resort principle; this is especially evident in the sudden attack on Yugoslavia. Hitler was irritated that the Yugoslav coup complicated his plans for invading Greece, so his attack on this nation looked more like a first rather than a last resort. To make matters worse still, the attacks showed no respect for the principle of discrimination. The Luftwaffe bombed Belgrade, among other cities, and in the process killed approximately 17,000 civilians.[7]

Hitler had another reason for invading Greece. In addition to protecting his flanks he was intent on rescuing Mussolini (Il Duce had invaded Greece in October of 1940).[8] But the invasion did not go well. After a while, the Greeks were on the offensive pushing the Italian armies back into Albania. Hitler's invasion turned things around quickly. In three weeks or so the German army had defeated the Greeks and forced their British allies to leave in a hurry. But as brilliant as the German invasion of Greece was militarily, it too violated the just cause, the last resort and the discrimination principles.

Finally, the Germans were ready to launch Barbarossa. They attacked on 22 June 1941. Their plan was to defeat the USSR with an overwhelming assault that would topple Stalin and his regime before the Russian winter set in.[9] To implement these plans, it was essential to surprise the Russians. In this respect Barbarossa was successful: Stalin was in a state of shock over what happened. He expected an attack at some future time, but not when it actually occurred. He thought that Hitler would not move against the USSR in the east until the British had been subdued in the west. Hitler, he thought, did not want a two-front war.

In effect, to achieve surprise, Hitler had to forgo following the principle of last resort. As a part of settling whatever disputes there were between Germany and the USSR by diplomacy, Hitler could have negotiated with Stalin and also, perhaps, set deadlines. But none of these resorts were tried. Instead there was a sudden and savage attack.

Just cause was also missing from the Barbarossa calculations. The Germans had not been attacked, nor were they about to be attacked. Nor had any German ally been attacked. Further, there were no humanitarian reasons for attacking the USSR. Actually there probably were. Stalin was already busy slaughtering many of his own people. But these reasons were not the kind to push Hitler into action. The Germans were simply interested in grabbing land and resources. Much of that land was due to be handed over to German nationals once the indigenous people had been expelled.[10] As to the resources of the conquered land, there was oil and food that could be exploited. Hitler felt Germany needed these resources if it was to maintain military supremacy in Europe over the long haul; The Third Reich after all was supposed to last for a thousand years.

The 'takeover' plan made it clear that the principle of discrimination would also not be honoured by the Germans. After a while, word got around among the Russian military that there was gross mistreatment of the populace and captured Russian soldiers. As a result, Russian resistance became fiercer. Many Russian soldiers felt that it would be better to stand and fight rather than be taken prisoner and then killed or starved to death in German prisoner-of-war camps. Of course, the Russian resistance stiffened not just because the Germans failed to follow the discrimination principle. Russian reinforcements came in from the Far East and new equipment manufactured east of the Urals, beyond the reach of the Luftwaffe, began to pour into the front. Equipment arriving from the US also helped. Further, the Germans themselves contributed to their own downfall. Planning as they did for a short war, they were unprepared for the Russian winter. One thing then led to another until the tide turned against the Germans at Stalingrad, and in front of Moscow and Leningrad.

JAPAN ATTACKS CHINA AND THE UNITED STATES

Japanese expansionist aspirations go back at least to the days of World War I. In those days, the Japanese were interested in sweeping up the remains of the German Empire in and around China.[11] Later in the 1920s and 1930s their aspirations led them into Manchuria and then back into China. Lacking many resources necessary for continuing their development as a modern nation, Japan quite naturally looked elsewhere for these resources. China especially showed promise for exploitation with an abundance of coal, cotton and various foodstuffs.[12] The exploitation took a serious turn when in 1937 an incident near Peking (Beijing), at the Marco Polo Bridge, started the Sino-Japanese War. As the war spread, the Japanese occupied most of north-east China, which included such cities as Peking, Nanking and Shanghai. They then moved down the coast past Canton, occupying key cities and locations so as to make it virtually impossible for China to communicate with the world via its eastern seaboard.

There is little question that Japan deserves the label of aggressor in this war. In no sense of the word did China threaten Japan. In the days prior to World War II, China was in no position to threaten any major power. She had for years been the object of aggression by the major colonial powers rather than an aggressor. Like these other powers, Japan was in China to take things from that large but largely underdeveloped land. It follows that Japan's intentions were also wrong. She could not possibly have acted from good intentions to satisfy just cause, because she had no just cause for going to war in the first place.

To be sure, Japan was in position in her war against China to satisfy some of the other principles of JWT. For one, she satisfied the legitimate authority principle. The proper authorities were certain leaders in Tokyo who either blessed what was happening in the field or directly authorized it. For another, Japan had a fighting chance to satisfy the likelihood of success principle. Although her army was relatively small, it was well trained and equipped. One can understand why the Japanese thought that they could gain whatever it is they wanted from China with relative ease. As it turned out, their optimism was unwarranted, since subjugating China proved to be no easy task. But, as has been noted already, the just war principles need to be assessed in terms of what was believed (rationally) before a war starts rather than after it is over. And, at the beginning, Japan could make a good case for believing that she would be successful.

As to the final two *jus ad bellum* principles, Japan clearly could not satisfy them. Proportionality could not be satisfied, because it was obvious from the beginning that her attack on China took place for the benefit of Japan alone. The cost and benefit analysis was in terms of self-interest. Had the analysis taken account of everyone's interests, the costs of the war (especially to the Chinese) would be seen to far exceed the benefits.

Last resort could not be satisfied either. It is true that the Japanese tried negotiating with the Chinese government, so they did not enter the war precipitously. But the negotiations seemed to be based on the principle 'what's mine is mine, what's yours is negotiable'. The Japanese never seriously offered to trade with the Chinese as a way of gaining what resources they needed to run their society. Instead, they short-circuited the process of reaching last (reasonable) resort by going to war.[13] So Japan violated most of the *jus ad bellum* principles. She probably also violated the *jus in bello* proportionality principle. Again there is little evidence to suggest that her military exhibited restraint in fighting the Chinese military. There is no question however that Japan violated the discrimination principle. Most infamously, her forces did so in Nanking where soldiers slaughtered between 100,000 and 200,000 civilians. Other cities and areas of China were ravaged as well. In responding to Chinese resistance, which often took the form of guerrilla war, the Japanese engaged in what they called a punitive campaign.[14]

In sum, the Japanese violated most of the principles of Just War Theory in their war with China. Their most serious violations appear to be of the just cause and discrimination principles.

Japan's aggressive tendencies in the years prior to the beginning of World War II were not limited to their weak western neighbour. At times, she looked north with an eye towards controlling the Communist threat from the USSR. At other times, she looked south to French Indochina, Singapore, the Philippines and the Dutch East Indies.

Eventually the southern strategy proved to be the more enticing. The time to strike seemed right, since France had been weakened by her defeat at the hands of the Germans in 1940 and was in no position to protect her Asiatic holdings. The Netherlands had also been weakened by war. As to the British, their military power was stretched to the limit protecting their homeland and Egypt. So in the whole area of Southeast Asia, there were few military forces strong enough to stop the Japanese once they started moving in that direction. The only force that could possibly have stoped them was stationed at Pearl Harbor. In theory, the US Navy could have moved from Pearl Harbor into the southwest to intercept any Japanese invasion force. So the Japanese had a good military reason for dealing with the US Navy.

They had another reason for taking action against the USA. In an attempt to curtail Japan's incursions in China, the USA had placed an embargo on scrap iron, steel, oil and other commodities that Japan needed; especially painful was the oil embargo.[15] The reaction of the Japanese to the sanctions was as if they were being strangled. In their eyes, it was the Americans who were the aggressors, while they were the victims. Also, as they saw it, if the USA refused to give them what they needed, they would simply get it by moving south.

But the Americans had to be taken care of, and soon. To wait risked having to face a much stronger US military down the road. Like France, Britain and the Netherlands, the US was relatively weak in 1941, so for the Japanese striking in 1941 was 'now or never'. And, as everyone knows, they chose 'now', and struck the Americans on 7 December.

Like their attacks on China, the Japanese did not have just cause on their side. They may have had grievances against the Americans, but none of these grievances could justify their attack on Pearl Harbor. Indeed, many of their grievances had to do with being denied access to materials that they could, and probably planned to, use to commit more acts of aggression. These are grievances that prevented the Japanese from reaching their self-interest goals. They had nothing to do with wider ethics. It follows that since they had mainly self-interested goals in mind, they not only violated the just cause principle but also the right intentions principle. What they did, they did intentionally – and what they did was triggered by bad intentions.

The last resort principle was also violated. Resorts such as warnings and deadlines were not tried. It is true that their intent was to deliver an ultimatum to Secretary of State Hull a few minutes before the bombs began to fall on Pearl Harbor,[16] but even if they had delivered the message in time, which they did not, the Americans would have had no time to respond before the war started. The ultimatum was an ultimatum in name only. It hardly represented a serious resort prior to the last resort of war.

As to proportionality it was violated almost by definition. The principle tells us that the good we do must be proportional to – that is, at least equal to or greater than – the harm we do. But if the Japanese were engaged in an unjust war, then that put them in a position of doing a great deal of harm. We can see this if we project what would have happened if the Japanese had been successful in their overall plans. The Japanese people would have been a happy lot, but hundreds of millions of people in China, Southeast Asia, the Philippines, and in Dutch East India would have been miserable.

The only two justice-of-the-war principles that Japanese satisfied in going to war with the USA, Britain, Australia and other allies is likelihood of success and legitimate authority. Success for the Japanese did not mean beating the USA with Japanese victory parades in Hollywood and Washington DC. That might have been the standard of success for a few Japanese leaders suffering from a touch of insanity. For others, success meant subjugating China, Southeast Asia and the islands in the western Pacific Ocean, and then convincing the Americans to let bygones be bygones.

Presumably the Americans would let the Japanese keep the lands they had won in war once they realized that they would suffer very heavy casualties in their effort to take back what the Japanese had won.

If that is what success meant back in 1941 before the war started, one would have to agree that there was some likelihood of success here. Historically, nations have become tired of war and, as a result, have come to agree to rather unpleasant arrangements that they would not have agreed to when their blood was up at the start of war. Before the conflict started, it was seen by the Japanese as unlikely that the Americans could sustain the instant rage they felt after the attack on Pearl Harbor. The conjecture was that it would wane in the face of heavy war casualties and, eventually, many people in the USA would start chanting 'bring the boys home'.

Satisfying the legitimate authority principle was easy for the Japanese. They had a strong government that controlled all decisions pertaining to war. So it was that government that planned for the war and then initiated it.

But what of *jus in bello* principles? Did the Japanese, in any significant way, honour the proportionality and the discrimination principles? The answer is no.[17] With respect to the latter principle, they exhibited a long record of attacking civilians. One example is what happened in Manila in the Philippines at the beginning of the war. General MacArthur had declared Manila to be an open city, but the Japanese bombed it anyway and in the process killed many civilians. That city suffered again near the end of the war. Perhaps as many as 100,000 civilians were killed in the battle for that city, with most of the deaths attributable to Japanese action. What happened to Manila was a carbon copy of what happened in many cities in China.

The Japanese were also guilty of mistreating prisoners. Many prisoners were killed, others were tortured and still others died or were seriously injured because they were forced to make long and exhausting marches or work in severely unhealthy conditions, without medical care and in overcrowded camps. American, British, Australian and other soldiers were many times more likely to die at the hands of their Japanese captors than in battle with them.

It is somewhat more difficult to assess Japanese behaviour with respect to the principle of proportionality (*in bello*). Early on in the war their military machine worked efficiently and probably caused only a little excessive harm to their enemies or to themselves. But late in the war, when they were gradually pushed back to their home islands, the Japanese began to violate the proportionality principle on a large scale. They did so by wasting the lives of their own military personnel with *banzai* charges. Here is an account of one of these charges.

> The last fight on Iwo Jima took place on the 26th of March [1945] while the 5th Division was preparing to come down from the hills and embark from the island. Members of the 531st Squadron were on their way to Airfield No. 2 when they noticed a few Japanese running across the road. In a matter of minutes about 300 Japanese were appearing as if from nowhere and had managed to overrun some US Garrison outfits and the 5th Division Pioneer Battalion. The Japanese were staging a final charge of destruction and confusion as they poured down upon the sleepy US troops. The battle was a mass of confusion as Marines, Army troops, and units from VII Fighter Command fought to stem the Japanese attack. The Japanese were armed with an assortment of US weapons as well as their own as they came out of their caves and holes in the ground.[18]

The attack caused American casualties so it cannot be said to have been a total waste for the attackers. Also, it and many other charges like it fall into the tradition of Japanese war ethics. *Bushido* asks Japanese soldiers not to surrender but, instead, to die in the name of the Emperor. Nonetheless, when these *banzai* charges are seen against the backdrop of Just War Theory, they represent a terrible waste of life. Typically in World War II, especially late in the war, the loss of life of Japanese personnel was grossly disproportional to the losses suffered by their enemies.

But what of the American participation in the Pacific war? Do the Americans fare any better than the Japanese as far as Just War Theory is concerned? They certainly do on the justice of the war side of that equation. They had just cause on their side not just because of the attack on Pearl Harbor – the Japanese had also attacked the Philippines and Wake Island. Japanese aggression was widespread, so a widespread response was called for. The Americans could and did argue that they were justified in launching a war to take back what they had lost and also to take their military forces to the source of the aggression. Since their intentions were driven mainly by just cause, the Americans could argue that they had good (right) intentions as well.

What about proportionality? Although everyone agreed that the Pacific war would be costly, the good that would come of it was said to outweigh the costs. Presumably some of the good had to do with returning lost lands. Good would also result from war if the Japanese government were weakened enough so that it could not resume its aggressive ways at some future time. Then there was the good of deterrence. Future potential aggressors would, presumably, be less likely to turn themselves into actual aggressors. Also to be placed on the balance sheet were the costs of not going to war. These included lives lost if the Japanese had permanently occupied China, Singapore, the Philippines, Indonesia, etc. Other costs included those of loss of freedom and losses due to exploitation. All these and other good effects and (avoidance of) bad ones were supposed to balance out the costs of the actual war in lives, property and infrastructure. The balancing meant that opponents of Japan could say that they had indeed satisfied the principle of proportionality.

Likelihood of success is more difficult to assess. Given the victories that the Japanese achieved in the first six months of the war (e.g., in the Philippines, Malaya, Singapore, Indonesia), it might seem that the likelihood of American (and Australian, etc.) success was pretty low and so the principle of success could not have been satisfied. However, from a longer perspective, a quite different picture emerges. Even the famous Japanese admiral Yamamoto realized that the industrial might of the USA would eventually overwhelm Japan. So he and his nation gambled on achieving a quick victory, and then gambled as well that the will of the USA would wane in the face of the high costs of continuing the war. Their gambles failed in part because they underestimated the will of the USA to right a wrong. But in assessing their own will, the Americans and their allies had good reason to believe that they would not waver and so they had good reason to believe that eventually the industrial might of the USA would, in fact, overwhelm the Japanese. So even though things looked quite bleak at first, the Americans and their allies could, and did, argue that they had a good overall chance of success.

The only other criterion to consider is legitimate authority. Here there was no problem. Once Japan struck and once Germany declared war on the USA, formal declarations of war were issued by the proper authorities. In effect, then, the USA satisfied all the *jus ad bellum* criteria of Just War Theory and can be said to have been fully justified in entering World War II.

What of the American record with respect to *jus in bello*? In fighting on the ground, their record is certainly superior to the Japanese. American soldiers treated prisoners, the wounded, the sick and civilians better than their enemy did. They did tend to be 'heavy on the trigger' and so, in many situations, caused more collateral damage than they probably should have. But it was in the air campaign that the Americans gained their greatest notoriety.

By the middle of 1944 the USA had occupied Saipan and the other Marianas islands. That put them in a position to begin a bombing campaign of Japan itself. The weapon they brought with them was the new Boeing B-29 bomber.[19] The B-29 was bigger, carried a heavier bomb load, flew farther and higher than any other World War II heavy bomber. It took the Americans a while to learn how best to utilize it. It turned out that bombing at high altitudes in daylight was not the best way to go. The main problem was that at high altitudes what later became known as the jet stream scattered the bombs hither and yon. The new commander of the bombing campaign, General Curtis LeMay, decided that the bombers would come in low over their targets and would fly at night. Since most of the buildings in Japanese cities were constructed of wood, he also decided that the weapons package his bombers would carry would include an ample supply of incendiaries. There was another advantage in this new way of attacking Japan. The Japanese did not have the same sophisticated night-fighting airplanes that the Germans had developed in their battle with Britain's RAF.

But in bombing at night, the RAF had learned that one cannot be overly concerned about hitting a particular factory or airport runway – one worries instead about finding the right city or town. By the early months of 1945, LeMay's bombers had learned their lesson well.

> On the night of March 9–10, 1945, LeMay sent 334 B-29 over Tokyo. Flying low, unarmed, and without having to stay in tight formations against fighter attacks, the big bombers showered a huge load of incendiaries on the Shitamachi section of Tokyo. The Japanese were caught by surprise, and their preparations to deal with large-scale fires were in any case hopelessly inadequate. For over three hours, the procession of B-29s lumbered over Tokyo, turning the great mixed area of homes and industry into a raging inferno. Between 80,000 and 100,000 died in the flames, which consumed some sixteen square miles of Tokyo's built up area in the raid which probably caused the largest number of casualties in World War II. Dozens of large factories and hundreds of feeder-workshops had been destroyed. A new stage of the air war against Japan had begun.[20]

For many World War II commentators, this and the many follow-on raids of Japanese cities such as Osaka, Kobe and Nagoya represent 'easy cases' of moral assessment. The principle of discrimination tells us that non-combatants should not be intentionally attacked; the Americans intentionally attacked non-combatants, so they did what they should not have done. End of assessment.

However, the assessment is not quite that simple and so probably does not belong in this chapter concerned with 'easy cases'. What complicates matters was the interspersing of military facilities within civilian areas of these cities. Given the absence of smart bombs, the Americans could only reach these factories, as they did, by causing a tremendous amount of collateral damage. Yet even with these complications, what the B-29s did to Japan in 1945 is still highly ethically suspect. Could, one wants to ask, the campaign have been conducted in some other way? What if the American bombers had flown low in the daytime? Could they have conducted an effective campaign at an acceptable casualty level?[21]

WAR IN KOREA – 1950–1953

After World War II, Korea was divided in two. The division was along the 38th parallel. The northern half would be controlled by the USSR, the southern half by the USA. Soon, a North Korean government was put in place that was sympathetic to the USSR. It was matched by a South Korean government sympathetic to the US. However, neither side was satisfied with this two-Koreas arrangement. Each side wanted to unify the nation under its own aegis and said so in the public arena. It didn't take long before verbal squabbles between the two Koreas led to violence. Both sides began shooting at each other on a regular basis,[22] and both were guilty of border incursions.

So when the North decided to invade the South, it was easy for the North's leaders to claim that South Korea was the aggressor. But similar to what happened in Poland in 1939, it was not difficult to identify who the real aggressor was. The South Korean military was in no condition to threaten the North. The United States had kept the South Korean military on a short leash in part because it did not trust Syngman Rhee, the South Korean president. He wanted to invade the North so he could unite his nation under his leadership.[23] Rhee was passionate about unification, and was willing to bring it about even if it meant war. He and many South Koreans were willing to risk war even after the American forces had exited Korea in 1948, leaving behind only a few advisors.

In contrast, North Korea was ready for war. She had been planning for it for some time, and had received the blessings of Stalin and Mao to go ahead with the invasion of the South.[24] In addition, the North Korean government had received military equipment from Russia, including a supply of T-34/85 1944 tanks.[25]

So when the war started on 25 June 1950, there was little question as to who the aggressor was and so who had not satisfied the principle of just cause. In addition to not satisfying that principle, the North Koreans did not satisfy the principle of last resort. The war started not so much because several forms of negotiations between the North and the South had been tried, but because the Americans had recently departed and the South was militarily weak. The North Koreans thus satisfied the likelihood of success principle: they knew that their chances were very good. The North Koreans also satisfied the proportionality principle. In their minds, they were in a position to win a quick victory. The war, they thought, would last less than a month. By then, their forces would be all the way south to the city of Pusan. They even planned to occupy the island of Cheju-do (off the southern coast of the peninsula) quickly by using local guerrilla forces sympathetic to their cause. So the war would not be costly, but the benefits of uniting Korea would be great. In the eyes of the North Koreans, then, they easily satisfied the principle of proportionality.

As to the two remaining *jus ad bellum* principles, the North Koreans satisfied one, but not the other. They clearly satisfied the legitimate authority principle. Kim Il Sung was the recognized leader of the North, with the authority to make decisions about war. But equally clearly the North did not satisfy the right intentions principle. The intentions of the North Korean leadership were to take over the southern half of the Korean peninsula and mould it into a communist nation like the North. This moulding was to the liking of some South Koreans, but not to the liking of most. This meant that the North Korean government would follow up its aggressive war policies by creating a government put in place by coercing the majority of the people in the South.

As to the South Korean government, it had the just cause principle on its side since it was the victim of massive aggression. The South had most of the other *jus ad bellum* principles on its side as well. The war was properly authorized by President Rhee and his government, and since their main intention was to repel the North Korean forces, it was a proper intention. Further, the last resort principle was moot given that the South had already been attacked. The South also satisfied the principle of proportionality. It could see that if it were successful in repelling the North, the benefits of going to war would be greater than the costs and submission to a communist regime. The only principle one might quibble about is likelihood of success. Given the relative strengths of the two sides, it might be thought that the South should simply have given up once attacked. However, it is not clear that the South fully appreciated how strong North Korea's military forces had become. In their minds, therefore, they probably thought that they had at least a fighting chance to resist the North and so were justified in putting up a fight.

Once the war started, the North Korean army advanced quickly into Seoul and from there further south. By 27 June, two days after the war began, the USA decided to enter. In a way, its entry was surprising. Months before (12 January), Secretary of State Dean Acheson had indicated in a speech before the National Press Club what the extent of the American defence perimeter was.[26] As it turned out, Korea was beyond the perimeter and would be expected, if attacked, to take care of itself. No doubt Acheson's speech encouraged Kim Il Sung to believe that if he attacked South Korea, the war would be an all-Korean affair.

Actually, the Americans did not enter the war alone. Many other nations contributed troops in the effort to stop the North Koreans; they all fought under the flag of the United Nations. On 27 June, the UN passed an American-sponsored resolution to 'furnish assistance' to the South Koreans.[27] But did all these nations and the UN enter the war in accord with JWT?

The just cause principle poses no problem for the combined forces. They acted to help an ally, friend or neighbour who was under attack. In doing so they satisfied one of the standard sub-principles of just cause: their intentions were on the side of the angels as well. Some of the participants may have had intentions in line with self-gain but, for the most part, it seems that the primary intention of the UN forces was to help rescue South Korea from an aggressor nation. Likewise, the likelihood of success principle was satisfied. It is true that there were close calls at the beginning of the war. The North Koreans came near to reaching Pusan even as the UN forces (mostly American) were deploying into the battlefields of Korea. Had the North Koreans taken Pusan, they would have captured the last port which could have been used to supply the South. But even though there were some scary moments, the UN command was justified in believing that its chances of stopping the North Koreans were good. The supply lines of the UN forces to the front lines got shorter as the North Koreans approached Pusan, while the North Korean lines got longer. Also, in the long run, the UN command must have calculated that its forces would overwhelm the North Koreans numerically.

What about proportionality? Well, again the UN forces are on the side of heaven. They figured (falsely as it turned out) that the costs of winning the war would not be overwhelming while the benefits of victory would be great. These benefits included stopping aggression, acting to deter future aggressors and saving the South Koreans from being ruled by a cruel political system.

As to last resort, there was little the UN could do about that principle. It did appeal to the North Koreans to stop their aggression before it decided to help the South. But beyond that it could not pursue further negotiations since the North Koreans were gobbling up large chunks of South Korean land by the day.

Finally, there is the legitimate authority principle to consider. Here again the UN, the USA, Great Britain and all the other countries that contributed personnel and supplies to help the South Koreans acted in accord of JWT. Each country entered the war with the blessing of its own legitimate authority, and the UN did so by a vote of the Security Council (minus the USSR, which was boycotting the UN on behalf of China).

American troops started streaming into Korea almost immediately upon declaration of war. The first troops were ill-prepared, ill-equipped and few in number. As a result, they were mauled by the well-trained and well-equipped North Korean army.[28] The South Korean troops were also battered. Both kept retreating, usually in disorder, until they formed the so-called Pusan perimeter. Once the UN forces had stabilized the situation, it became possible to think about counter-attacking the North Koreans.

The counter-attack was very dramatic; it featured landings at Inchon, located just west of Seoul.[29] These landings were risky enough to generate opposition among UN military commanders and many political leaders. But the overall UN commander in Korea, General Douglas MacArthur, argued that outflanking the North Korean forces ranged around Pusan to the south would in the long run be less costly than slogging back up the Korean peninsula one mile at a time. In the terminology of JWT, MacArthur argued that it would have been disproportionate (*in bello*) not to land behind the North Koreans at Inchon.

The landings, on 15 September 1950, were very successful and, soon, Seoul was liberated.[30] After that, the UN forces decided to move north of the 38th parallel. In fact, they attempted to move all the way into North Korea to the Yalu River and thereby use the war as an occasion to unify the peninsula. Unfortunately, this move alarmed China. Also regrettable was the fact that MacArthur had deployed his troops poorly in the drive to the north. The 8th Army moved north on the western side of the peninsula, while the newly formed X Corp (composed of both army and marine units) moved up along the eastern side. The problem was that there was a mountainous gap between these two forces of almost 200 miles. When the Chinese decided to enter the war under the just cause banner of helping an ally in distress, they moved through the gap. They came to Korea in such large numbers that they swept the UN forces back down the peninsula all the way through to Seoul and beyond.

Demoralized, it seemed for a while that the UN forces would be driven off the peninsula completely; but under a new operational commander, General Matthew B. Ridgeway, they pulled themselves together. By the middle of March 1951 Seoul was retaken and the UN forces moved farther north to a line that in places is below and at other places above the 38th parallel. A stalemate ensued. Many died after that, as both sides fought for this or that mountain top. But there was very little movement on the ground in the last year or so of the war. Eventually, on 27 July 1953, an armistice was signed.

Here are some comments about the ethics of the war that, so far, have not been covered. I discuss them serially to help keep the narrative from becoming overly lengthy.

1. The Chinese probably satisfied all of the *jus ad bellum* JWT principles. It has already been noted that they had just cause on their side in so far as they were helping an ally. But last resort is in evidence too: they had no choice but to act lest all of Korea got swallowed up by the imperialist-led UN forces. The war was properly authorized by Mao and the Chinese leadership; they had the good intentions of undoing the harm done to the North Koreans. They also had a high likelihood of success on two counts: one, they figured that they had an excellent chance of pushing the UN forces away from the Chinese border and, two, a good chance of restoring the status of the North Korean government to something like its *ante-bellum* state. Of course, if they also had the intention of uniting all of Korea under the red banner, their likelihood of success was small.
2. The North Koreans, probably more than the Chinese, violated the principle of discrimination.[31] There were numerous occasions when North Korean soldiers killed prisoners and civilians

who were thought to be sympathetic to the government of Syngman Rhee.

3. Evidently the South Korean forces were ruthless in dealing with their enemies. For example, troops were sent in to subdue a Communist-led rebellion on the island of Cheju-do. In the process, much of the island was laid waste and the inhabitants suffered approximately 60,000 casualties.[32]
4. UN forces were not totally innocent of violating the principle of discrimination. Lack of discipline in many cases led to vandalism, murder and rape.[33]
5. The UN (specifically the US Air Force) also violated the principle of discrimination. Late in the war, it engaged in bombing raids on North Korean cities and towns to rival the raids of World War II.[34] If the war had continued, there was hardly have been a target available worth the price of the bombs being dropped on it.
6. The Chinese, but also the North Koreans, were probably guilty of violating the proportionality principle. Their mass attacks on UN forces led to excessive loss of life among their own forces.

CLOSING THOUGHTS

These are easy cases for Just War Theory. They are not easy because everyone agrees with the analyses of the cases presented in this chapter. The hope is, however, that most do agree. If there is agreement, at least in a rough and ready way, JWT gains some credibility. But theories are supposed to deal with not-so-easy cases as well as easy cases. The next chapter takes up some of these harder cases to see how well JWT deals with them.

5 Harder Cases: Serbia, Russia, Kosovo, Iraq

SERBIA 1914

Just War Theory can be used either prospectively or retrospectively. It is probably used in the latter way more frequently than the former – after all, assessing the past is easier than assessing a murky future. Assessing the past is also more satisfying to many, especially if the assessment allows them to second-guess leaders and politicians that they are not particularly fond of.

The previous chapter presented cases retrospectively. These cases were presented not primarily as history; the idea was to show that it was possible to make judgements using Just War Theory and to make these judgements with relative ease. What the leaders during World War II actually thought they were doing was not central to the plan of the presentation. The fact that these leaders may never have heard of JWT, or may never have accidentally made decisions in accord with it, does not affect the main idea of the chapter – that JWT can be used successfully in a wide variety of cases. How wide is not yet clear. At this point, one can't help but wonder: can the theory be used more widely so as to apply to harder cases? That question is tackled here in four quite different hard cases.

The first concerns World War I. This war poses more problems for the theory because of the just cause principle. Clear-cut cases of aggression and response to that aggression were rare during that war; the German invasion of Belgium is perhaps an exception.

Once the war started, and the Germans found themselves at war with France, they were intent on implementing their so-called Schlieffen Plan. This plan, devised by Field Marshal von Schlieffen in the late nineteenth century, was supposed to help German forces move around the main French defences to the south by going through the south-east corner of Belgium. So prior to their invasion of France, the Germans asked the Belgians for free passage through their country.[1] The Belgians refused to give permission, as they had every right to do. They were promptly invaded. Belgium clearly had just cause on its side whereas Germany, clearly the aggressor, did not.

England too had just cause on her side. Officially she acted in defence of Belgium with whom she had a treaty promising aid if Belgium happened to be attacked by the monster nation to the east.

Still, many nations that entered the war did so under conditions that made it difficult to know whether they had just cause on their side. A case in point is Austria-Hungary. She was not attacked either by the Serbian or the Russian armies, her potential enemies. But on 28 June, Archduke Franz Ferdinand and his wife were assassinated in Sarajevo. The assassin was Gavrilo Princip who had earlier made his way from Serbia into Bosnia and then to Sarajevo. Princip was an ethnic Serb, but also an Austrian citizen. Evidently, he had received help in what he did from some Serbian source.[2] He and his several associates had obtained guns from that source and were also helped in their sojourn to Sarajevo. Further, they knew that the Archduke would be in Sarajevo when they arrived, as the Archduke's itinerary had been announced well in advance.[3]

The source of the help that Princip and his friends received was most likely Colonel Dimitrievich. He was the 'Chief of the Intelligence Section of the Serbian General Staff and head of the terrorist society known as the "Black Hand,". . ..'[4] If indeed Dimitrievich was the source, the question is: did the Archduke's murder constitute an act of aggression and so give

Austria-Hungary just cause for starting a war against Serbia? On the negative side it could be argued that the Serbian government did not *officially*, or even unofficially, authorize the assassination. Very likely, few in the Serbian government knew anything about the plot. Officially, then, the government could lament the loss of the Archduke with diplomatic sincerity; what members of the government might have felt privately is another matter. Since, the argument continues, the Serbian government had nothing to do with the assassination, it would be unjust for Austria-Hungary to attack Serbia.

On the positive side, one focus of the argument is on the seriousness of the act. The Archduke was, after all, the heir apparent to the throne of Austria-Hungary. It was not as if Princip had killed some minor functionary of the Austrian-Hungarian Empire – he struck a blow at the heart of the empire.[5] The other focus is on Serbian complicity. An important Serbian government official was, after all, the primary suspect behind the plot. And even if no one else in the government besides Dimitrievich was involved, it still falls on that government to take collective responsibility for what happened. It was up to that government, even if it could not stop the killing, at least to do all it could to punish those really responsible. Since not much was done, Serbia deserves blame and thus deserves the label of aggressor.

A case, then, can be made on either side concerning just cause. As to Just War Theory, it is not of much help in deciding which side to favour because of the vague way in which the just cause principle is usually stated. Not being a legal document with some court behind it to interpret its meaning, it is pretty much left to each 'victim' nation to decide when and if it is suffering from aggression. No doubt, it can be 'second-guessed' at that time and later by other nations, academics, social critics and others. Still, in 1914, the decision as to how to interpret just cause rested with the government of Austria-Hungary.

For that government, the decision was easy to make. Before the assassination, Austria-Hungary and Serbia had been feuding over various matters in the Balkans, including the status of Bosnia. Austria-Hungary had recently made Bosnia part of its empire. Serbia and various ethnic groups within Bosnia wanted Bosnia to become part of greater Serbia or be allowed to become independent. So emotions were high all round; there was even talk of war before the Archduke's assassination. The killing, then, could only inflame emotions that were already almost out of control. As it turned out, these emotions did not immediately lead to war, even though the actions of Austria-Hungary suggested that it was spoiling for a fight.

Soon after the assassination, Austria-Hungary asked for, and got, reassurance from Germany that it would receive support should war start. Later – almost a month later, in fact – Austria-Hungary sent an ultimatum to Serbia, asking that nation to meet a series of conditions if it wished to avoid war.

> Serbia was required to suppress all propaganda directed against the Monarchy, to dissolve *Narodna Obrana* [National Defence, a society dedicated to a return of lost Serbian provinces], to remove from the Army and administration such persons as the Austrian Government might stipulate, to arrest certain individuals, to punish severely frontier officials involved in illegal activity, and most important 'to accept the collaboration in Serbia of representatives of the Austro-Hungarian Government for the suppression of subversive movement directed against the territorial integrity of the Monarchy'.[6]

The ultimatum hardly represented a serious attempt at avoiding war since its conditions were nothing less than humiliating. The Serbs could only turn it down and thus come face to face with war.

Space does not allow for a full discussion of all the Just War Theory criteria implicated in the confrontation between Austria-Hungary and Serbia. But enough has been said to make it clear that there are difficulties, if not with applying last resort, then with the just cause principle. More difficulties can be found, again especially with just cause, when other nations enter what became known as World War I.

RUSSIA AND GERMANY, 1914

The problem facing the major powers in Europe was how they could localize the war between Austria-Hungary and Serbia. Given the many agreements and commitments that the major European powers had with each other, localizing conflict would not be easy. Russia was bound to Serbia to give assistance were Serbia to be attacked, and Germany was bound to Austria-Hungary in a similar way. Further, France was on Russia's side. The idea was to squeeze Germany between two powers so that she would be reluctant to go to war on two fronts. England too was in the mix. In addition to a commitment to help Belgium, she had an understanding to support France were she to be attacked.

In spite of these intertwining commitments, a *prima facie* case can be made that Russia had just cause on her side in favour of war. Her ally, Serbia, was in fact attacked so that she could be portrayed as living up to her commitments. But the case for helping Serbia was not as strong as it seems. To be sure, JWT tells us that a nation is supposed to help when its ally is being attacked. But the commitment to help does not necessarily apply when the ally is, or probably is, the aggressor.

As has been already noted, Serbia may or may not have been an aggressor. In the eyes of the Russians she probably was not – she was the victim. So the Russians might be excused for threatening Austria-Hungary and excused as well for eventually going to war with he. However they certainly knew something about Serbian involvement in the Archduke's assassination. They would have, or should have, seen the judgement of going to war against Austria-Hungary as a close call.

Even beyond the issue of war with Austria-Hungary, Russia knew well that war against her would more than likely lead to war against Germany. But as Austria-Hungary moved its forces south to be in position to attack Serbia, it left its borders with Russia to the north and east exposed. That in turn put pressure on the Germans to bear the main responsibility for protecting the whole of the eastern front from a Russian attack, a responsibility that Germany could not easily bear. After all, part of the German army faced west towards France. Since what Germany most feared was war on two fronts, it would have preferred that the Austro-Hungarian army give it as much help as possible. The last thing that Germany wanted was to have the Austro-Hungarian army 'go south' away from the Russian front.

It was particularly distressing to Germany when Russia began to talk about mobilizing its armed forces.[7] Mobilizing a large military force takes time. It means calling all reserves into service, cancelling leave for those called up, manning front-line fortifications, mining harbours and the like. It also means getting ready for war so that the other side is at a great disadvantage if it does not itself mobilize. For a while, the Russians dithered. They couldn't decide whether partly or fully to mobilize – or whether to mobilize at all Eventually, by the end of July, they mobilized fully. They did so even though the Germans were in no position to threaten them. The Germans, after all, were stretched thin since they could not count on receiving much help from the Austro-Hungarians. Understandably, Germany tried to get Russia to reverse its mobilization. Its ultimatum ignored, Germany decided not only to mobilize but to go to war with Russia.[8]

What sort of Just War Theory credit or discredit does Russia receive for becoming involved in war in 1914? It was, in fact, Germany that got Russia into the war: Germany declared war on Russia. Russia, then, appears to be the victim of German aggression. But it was the Russian move to mobilize that triggered the German response. That piece of foolishness represented yet another step down the slide to a world war. The Germans could have simply responded with a counter-mobilization; they need not have taken the step of actually starting a war. But the atmosphere in July 1914 was charged with emotion, so the Russians must have known that their mobilization was highly likely to trigger a violent response. So although, again, the issue is not clear-cut, it would appear that the Russians deserve marks of discredit for taking steps that led to war. Putting it differently, they deserve much of the discredit for keeping the war between the Austrian-Hungarian Empire and Serbia from remaining local.

What about the Germans? What credit or discredit do they deserve? In one sense, the Germans were victims. They certainly viewed themselves as such. Had the Russians not forced their hand in July 1914, there is a good chance that the larger war involving the major powers in Europe would not have started. But, in another sense, their hand was not forced to the extent that they had to declare war on Russia. They could have counter-mobilized, and then waited to see what might transpire. Instead, they began mobilizing and then quickly declared war on Russia.

But they did more than that. They also declared war on France soon after they began mobilizing against that country. Why? They had two reasons. First, the Germans knew that the agreement between Russia and France meant that to be at war with one meant being at war with the other. So going to war with France was less a matter of aggressing against her as a case of facing reality. Given the situation, war with France was unavoidable. Second, and more important, Germany was facing enemies both to its east and west. What she needed was a plan to deal with the problem. The Schlieffen Plan, mentioned above, fitted the bill. The plan called for a swift march through Belgium and an equally swift, and decisive, campaign against France. The idea was to deal with France before the cumbersome but massive Russian army was fully ready for war. The policy was to hold the east in place, deal with the west, and then fight a single-front war against the Russians in the east. So Germany was probably thinking in terms of 'getting on with it' before her enemies had gathered momentum.

Given, then, that Germany started two wars, one against Russia and one against France, it would appear that she did not have just cause on her side. Germany had more the look of an aggressor than a victim of aggression. But notice how less clear-cut the issue is when what Germany did in 1914 is compared with what she did in 1939 against Poland, in 1940 against Denmark and Norway and in 1941 against Yugoslavia, Greece and the USSR. With all these wars, one would be hard pressed to give one good (just) reason for them. German actions in these wars represent gross violations of just cause. But what Germany did in 1914 was not gross. In truth, some government officials, including the Kaiser, made efforts to keep a wider war from starting. Further, with Russia mobilizing, Germany's war declarations give the appearance of being defensive rather than offensive gestures. So although Germany's acts of war are still unjust, they are less unjust than they might have been.

One can arrive at the same conclusion by considering how the principle of last resort played out in 1914. Germany's entrance into the war was not premeditated in the way Barbarossa was in 1941 – there was no well-in-advance set date to go to war as with Hitler's invasion of Russia. In 1914, various efforts were made to stop the slide to what would become World War I.[9] Those efforts were not especially well planned so, in the end, Germany found herself gradually descending into war. Various resorts were tried to avoid war, even if none could reasonably count as the resort prior to the last resort of war. So, again, Germany failed to meet one of the criteria of Just War Theory, but it did so more by degrees rather than in a gross or blatant manner.

France was, by degrees also, complicit. Late in July she was pressuring Russian officials in St Petersburg to mobilize the Russian military.[10] The Russian military attaché in Paris was also pressured. It was as if these French officials either wanted a war but wanted someone else to precipitate it, or that they did not fully comprehend the consequences of their recommendations to the Russians. Whatever the case, in the end, the Germans declared war on France and then proceeded to invade her by implementing the Shlieffen Plan. So France had just cause on her side, even if that cause was somewhat tainted.

Britain's entry in the war was not tainted. Although she was tempted in the direction of war by potential gains of German colonies if she won, she entered the war to help defend her allies – in the first instance Belgium. Britain also had a commitment to help France if she were attacked, as she was. So of the major powers to enter the war in 1914, Britain is the only one that does not constitute a difficult case.

More could be said about how Just War Theory plays out in World War I. For example, much could be said of the (im)morality of the British naval blockade of Germany, and Germany's retaliatory submarine blockade of Britain. Then there are questions about how the Austro-Hungarian armies treated Serbian civilians, and how German soldiers treated Belgian civilians. But space does not permit going into all these details. It is enough for the present to show that Just War Theory can deal with certain kinds of hard cases, at least in a rough and ready way, and then move on to other cases to see how it can deal with them.

KOSOVO, 1999

The challenge the war in Kosovo poses for Just War Theory is quite different from that of World War I, even though there are some similarities. One similarity has to do with just cause. In both wars, some of the participants did not have a clear-cut just cause for starting a war. One of the differences concerns legitimate authority. With World War I, there were no arguments about who should authorize the beginning of war; but in Kosovo there was. Some background is needed to see how these similarities and differences play out.

Like so many wars, trouble was brewing in Kosovo long before conflict broke out. Kosovo is located in the southwestern portion of former Yugoslavia. By the mid- to late twentieth century, it was populated mostly by Muslim migrants from Albania. Gradually other people, including the ruling Christian (Orthodox) Serbs, were pushed out. By the time of the 1999 crisis, 90 per cent of the Kosovar population was Muslim.[11]

What precipitated the crisis was that the Kosovars were given extensive autonomy within Serbia in 1974, but then had much of that autonomy taken away in 1989. At first, under the leadership of Ibrahim Rugova, the reaction to this loss was non-violent. Rugova was the leader of the Democratic League of Kosovo (LDK). Other nations and peoples, he thought, would respond more positively to his cause if violence were avoided. But, predictably, as Rugova proved unable to deliver autonomy to his people, other Kosovars became restless and began to resort to sporadic violence. Gradually, throughout the 1990s, the violence increased. At first it was aimed at the Serbian police forces. Later, some Serbian civilians were attacked. Evidently the aim was to coerce the remaining Serb minority into leaving Kosovo. In effect, the attackers were attempting to practise ethnic cleansing. Most of these attacks were sponsored by the Kosovo Liberation Army (KLA). The KLA was far more impatient than the LDK in demanding a return of political power to the Kosovar people. In fact, the KLA wanted powers far beyond those revoked in 1989. It demanded that Kosovo become a completely independent nation.

The Serbians responded to the Kosovar provocation. They attacked Kosovar villages using their version of ethnic cleansing. Murder, rape and the destruction of property were common. Given that the Serbs had regular military and organized police forces, their ethnic cleansing, in what was now a guerrilla war, was more extensive than the KLA's. As a result, thousands of refugees left villages and towns and headed for the mountains or the Albanian border.

The rest of the world took note of what was happening. It did so because there was vivid television coverage of the events in Kosovo. There were also many reporters who wrote about the grisly atrocities, especially those committed by the Serbs. It seemed to many, then, that a humanitarian disaster was in the making, and that someone should be doing something about it. As it turned out, NATO decided that it should be the one to act.

But there were questions about the news coverage. It seemed to some that the coverage exaggerated the extent of the atrocities; its very vividness made matters seem worse than they were.

No doubt deaths numbered in the thousands – two, three or four.[12] And that is serious enough. But the news coverage made it seem as if the numbers were much larger. In their excessive excitement over what was happening in Kosovo, Europeans and Americans may have thought they had a strong just-cause case for war when, in fact, their case may not have been so strong.

If mass media reports distorted NATO judgements about just cause, these same reports also distorted their proportionality judgements. The proportionality principle is supposed to weigh the costs versus the benefits of war. However, if the benefits of Kosovars (and Serbs) being saved by NATO's intervention were less than was imagined, then the expected costs of war would weigh more heavily in the final analysis. In other words, the good of going to war could very well be overridden by the costs (of bombing Kosovo and Serbia).

So when one looks at the Kosovo crisis more dispassionately than many people did in 1999, it is not so clear how the two principles of just cause and proportionality played out. It may be that these two principles were not satisfied quite so completely as some NATO cheerleaders might have supposed.

The decision to have NATO act in Kosovo created another problem. This time the principle affected was legitimate authority. To many, it hardly seemed appropriate for NATO, an organization whose purpose is the defence of Western Europe, to attack a nation that was not threatening it or any of its members. To them, the real legitimate authority was the United Nations. Although the UN had passed a resolution (1199) saying that the Kosovo situation was a threat to peace and security, it had not uttered the magic words 'all necessary means' to legitimize the use of force to end the crisis.[13] The reason these words were not used was that Russia (and China) would have vetoed them in the Security Council. This meant that the UN was limited to using political pressure – words – to stop the chaos that was developing in Kosovo. Unfortunately the chaos continued in spite of all the talk in and around UN headquarters.

One of the most dramatic examples of the slide into chaos occurred in Racak on 15 January 1999. There were claims and counterclaims about what happened, but what is undisputed is that there were 45 dead ethnic Albanians. The Serbs claimed that those killed were KLA members or civilians caught in the cross-fire of a skirmish with the KLA. But Human Rights Watch very quickly rejected this interpretation.[14] They interviewed witnesses (who had been hiding) whose testimony indicated that the Racak incident was well planned and executed by the Serbs. Human Rights Watch also obtained recordings of telephone conversations between Serbian officials 'who clearly ordered government security forces to "go heavy" in Racak. Two officials later discussed ways that the killings might be covered up to avoid international condemnation'.[15]

These and similar events convinced NATO that if the UN could not act, it must do so. So NATO made the highly disputable claim that it could act as a legitimate authority for resolving the conflict between the Serbs and Kosovars. The problem here is that the legitimate authority principle does not tell us how to decide which extra-national political entity is the legitimate authority. It is left up to the political entities themselves to legislate the transfer of legitimacy to larger political entities such as NATO or the UN. But even when the transfer is effected through international laws, it is difficult to tell how seriously it is to be taken. Do political entities such as nations really mean to transfer their legitimacy to an organization (with all its laws, resolutions, etc.) that they have little influence over and that does not have the power in hand to enforce its authority? There is enough ambiguity in the transfer process to encourage disagreement as to the justice of the NATO decision to use NATO itself as the instrument that would bypass the UN. That decision – taken by a large group of nations and not just by one maverick nation – shows that the legitimate authority problem is serious indeed.

Once the war started, one other major challenge to JWT emerged. NATO fought the war almost exclusively from the sky. It thought that the Serbs and their leader Slobodan Milošović could be forced to submit as a result of a robust bombing campaign. To make sure that it followed the principle of discrimination, NATO made extensive use of smart weapons. However, because NATO was keen to keep its own casualties as low as possible, its bombing raids were launched from 15,000 feet. Inevitably, at that altitude, mistakes were made. What from a great height looked like a Serbian army convoy occasionally turned out to be a column of refugees instead. In no sense of the word was NATO aiming at civilian targets, so it was not guilty of attacking civilians the way the Serbian forces and the KLA were. Nonetheless, it killed civilians in some numbers by mistake.

What made things look bad was that these killings could have been avoided. Had the NATO planes come in lower, fewer mistakes would have been made. Things looked bad as well because the high-altitude bombing policy made it seem as if NATO airmen (and their airplanes) were more valuable than the people on the ground whom NATO was supposed to be saving.

A second problem emerged late in the bombing campaign. In the minds of the NATO attackers, the Serbs should have capitulated after two, three, maybe four weeks of bombing. But they did not. Serb stubbornness warranted extending the campaign; that is what NATO did. It ran the bombing campaign into a fifth and sixth week. But even that was not enough. So enlarged target lists were extended into Serbia itself. Now various dual-use infrastructure targets were fair game: bridges, roads, railroad tracks, power plants, radio and television towers, civilian airports as well as scores of other targets were hit.[16] In effect, NATO airpower brought the war home to the Serbs and did the job. After eleven weeks of bombing, the Serbian government capitulated to NATO's demands.

It is difficult to come up with an overall assessment of the bombing campaign in terms of the principle of discrimination. When one focuses on NATO's high-altitude bombing policy and its extended bombing campaign, there is a tendency to condemn NATO and leave it at that. When, however, one focuses on the care taken in selecting targets and the heavy use of smart weapons, NATO appears to deserve praise. In the end, NATO probably deserves a mixed report card. Certainly NATO's card, however tainted, is nowhere near as bad as the cards of the Serbian military or the KLA.

WAR IN IRAQ 2003

On the face of it, the war in Iraq is not a hard case for Just War Theory. One can argue rather easily that the invaders did not have just cause for that war. In 2003, Iraq was not an aggressor as it had been in 1980 against Iran and 1990 against Kuwait. Nor, at that time, was Iraq engaged in crimes against humanity. Earlier, in the last year of the war with Iran, Iraq had used chemical weapons against the Kurds in order to curb their rebelliousness and, perhaps, to punish them for cooperating with Iran. Also, right after the war in Kuwait, the Iraqi government had ruthlessly put down a Shi'ite revolution in the southern part of the country. In 2003, however, Iraq was not causing humanitarian catastrophe; no one was in a position to justify intervening in Iraq in order to stop aggression or an ongoing humanitarian disaster.

Nor was any nation in a position to argue that it had just cause to attack because Iraq possessed weapons of mass destruction. As it turned out, no such weapons were found prior to the war and after the invasion. But even if there had been such weapons, it was clear that the Iraqis were not about to use them. Their military machine had taken a severe blow during the Gulf War of 1991 and had not yet recovered. No one believed that Iraq was in position to start a major war in 2003 or 2004, so no nation or group of nations could claim that it was justified in invading Iraq as an act of preemption. Had the weapons been there, a preventive reason could have been given for the attack. Maybe four or five years hence Saddam would have been able to mount a major attack on Iran, Saudi Arabia or even Kuwait. But, as was made clear in

Chapter 2, such a reason is not allowed by the just cause principle. Preemption yes, prevention no.

One other just-cause-like reason was given to justify the invasion of Iraq. It was said, mostly by the neo-conservatives in America, that is was the duty of the sole superpower still in existence to spread democracy around the world and that, if need be, do the job violently;[17] so tyrants who stand in the way of democratization should be overthrown. Saddam Hussein was a tyrant and so had to be overthrown.

The trouble with this argument is that Just War Theory has no room for it. The theory says that wars are not just if they are started for ideological reasons. Starting a war to spread Islam, Christianity, fascism, communism or even democracy is just not allowed. So, again, to say that the main purpose of the Iraq invasion was (is) to spread democracy is not to present a proper just cause to the discussion.

In the end, then, applying the just cause principle to the Iraq War turns that war into an easy rather than a hard case. The same is true when the last resort principle is applied to that war. It is true that (sincere?) efforts were made to avoid war before hostilities actually started. Many UN resolutions were passed prior to the final one, 1441, claiming that Iraq was still in material breach of other resolutions and that if it did not change its ways there would be 'serious consequences'.[18] It is also true that efforts were made to pass an additional resolution that would more explicitly authorize the use of force to gain compliance. Other efforts were also made. So those who went to war with Iraq did so not as a first, second or even third resort. Still, it was known at the time that Iraq was militarily much weaker than it was in 1991. Even though it was obvious that Iraq was stalling for time, time was still on the side of her enemies. They could have waited at least for a year or two before, in total frustration, they needed to act. Thus a rather easy case can be made for saying that the last resort principle was also violated when the 2003 invasion of Iraq began.

In view of the apparent ease with which Just War Theory can show that the Iraq War is unjust, how can it be argued that that war presents a hard case for that theory? Not easily! But that is the job of the next chapter. It aims to show how and why the war in Iraq is indeed a hard case for Just War Theory.

6 Multiple Reasons

SINGULAR AND MULTIPLE REASON GIVING

In Chapter 1, various theories in ethics were said to fall within the framework of exceptions theory. These theories help tell us when we can make exceptions to rules of ethics that we all agree on. 'Yes, of course, I am not supposed to lie but, in this case, not to lie to the terrorist is likely to result in a catastrophe. So I lie, but I do so justly'. Put differently, I have a good reason to lie.

Similarly, one nation has a good reason to engage in battle with a neighbour when that neighbour is attacking it. The reason for going to war here is not just good – theory tells us that it is sufficiently good. It is such a good reason that no additional reason is required. Other reasons, sufficient ones perhaps, might be available but they are not needed. It is the same with a humanitarian catastrophe. It is enough, by itself, to justify an invasion if such a catastrophe is taking place. And it is enough, by itself, to justify a preemptive strike if a belligerent neighbour state is in the final throes of readying an attack by loading its strike airplanes with bombs, placing artillery shells next to guns located near the front and moving troops up to the border.

As it is traditionally conceived, then, just cause is more often than not presented as a single cause. What one looks for in justifying going to war is a single sufficient just cause. Having that one cause, and satisfying the other just war principles as well, a nation can go to war with a good conscience.

There is nothing wrong with single-cause reasoning. Many of our decisions, both in war and everyday life, fit that pattern of thinking. Mary is terribly rich. For Aaron, who loves money, nothing else matters – he will marry her. But Jim, who is also contemplating marriage, is attracted to Betty for many reasons; there is no single one that has prompted him to ask for her hand. Betty has a nice smile and that counts for something. So does her personality that makes everyone around her to feel warm and welcome. There is also the good taste she exhibits in how she dresses and presents herself in public. And so on. No one of these reasons leads him to propose marriage to Betty and, perhaps, no two of them do. But together they make Betty irresistible to Jim.

When it comes to deciding about war one wants to ask: why is the just cause principle in JWT thought of primarily in terms of a single cause (i.e., as singular)? Here is one answer. War is a tragic business. Many people die in war, and many more are seriously hurt. To justify going to war a nation needs not just a reason but an overriding one. A small single good reason is not enough. Nor is it enough to give a second small reason, or a third one.

In reply, it can be argued that several small reasons can, in theory, rise to the level of a single overriding reason. The whole might not be greater than the sum of the parts, but the parts may add up to a single overriding reason.

Applied to the Iraq War, this sort of multiple-reasons thinking could be used to try to make a case for saying that the coalition forces had just cause – that is, they had a string of just (or good) reasons for going to war. Here is a candidate list of such reasons as it might have been expressed by supporters of that war before it started.

1. Saddam is today, as he has been ever since he came to power, a tyrant. As a tyrant, he is persecuting a wide variety of people. Even if this persecution does not at present rise to the level of a 'humanitarian catastrophe' it is still extremely serious. Or, to

put it in terms that the ancient Chinese philosopher Mo Tzu (who wrote about the ethics of war) would have understood, because of his bad behaviour, Saddam has lost his mandate of Heaven.[1]

2. Saddam and his government are in material breach of UN resolutions, but most especially 1441. Although the Iraqis have allowed UN inspectors into Iraq on two separate occasions after the 1991 war, the access to facilities that might contain weapons of mass destruction was rarely 'free and unfettered'.
3. Saddam and his government are engaged in creating and deploying weapons of mass destruction. (Of course, this reason was earlier discounted to 'zero' in the framework of Just War Theory because a response to the presence of these weapons is a preventive, not a preemptive, measure. So the presence of these weapons cannot be used as a sufficient reason for starting a war. But there is nothing to prevent using the argument as a contributing reason. After all, these weapons are more dangerous today than in the past and so they should not be completely discounted as part of the just-cause reasoning process.)
4. He and/or some individuals within the Iraqi government attempted to assassinate George Bush when the former president visited Kuwait in 2002.
5. The Iraqis never completely complied with the Gulf War ceasefire agreement of 1991. So, in a sense, the war of 2003 is simply a continuation of the 1991 war.
6. Since the 1991 conflict, the Iraqis have made war on the Kurds in the north of Iraq and the Shi'ites in the south. They have killed many civilians. These abuses forced western coalition partners to designate certain areas of Iraq as no-fly zones for Iraqi planes. In response, the Iraqis have fired on coalition airplanes on numerous occasions.
7. The Iraqis have been and are still supporting terrorists in the Middle East in various ways.

COMPLAINTS

What is going on here with this form of reason giving? Two things. Together they imply that the just cause principle needs to be modified. The first, as already stated, has to do with introducing the concept of multiple-reasons thinking to the theory. Although no one of the above reasons may be considered sufficient by war supporters to trigger a war in Iraq, perhaps a combination of three or four of them might be. The second involves allowing a wider variety of good reasons (just causes) into the final calculation of just cause than does the standard theory. In this connection, the actual list of good reasons above is not what is important. In fact, the list looks suspiciously like a portion of the neo-conservative agenda. What is important is not the list itself, but that some list or other can be created to develop an overall just cause sufficiently strong to justify war.

Two complaints are likely to emerge from this different view of just cause. First, the modification complicates assessments of just cause. Unmodified or standard Just War Theory has a relatively easy time determining whether a nation has a just cause or not. It is true that just cause under the standard theory is itself subject to vagueness. It is not always clear, for example, whether a raid by a small group of enemy soldiers constitutes aggression or not. What if the attacking group is a company of soldiers backed by artillery? What if two companies attack? When does the attack come to count as an act of aggression? Yet in spite of such vagueness, the list of causes that helps tell us that a nation has a just cause is limited. By the count accepted in Chapter 2, it comes down to six (a nation is responding to an ongoing attack; it is responding to a recent attack; it is acting preemptively; it is defending an ally being attacked now; it is defending one that was attacked recently; and it is acting to stop a humanitarian disaster). But under the modified version of the just-cause concept the list becomes open-ended and so overcomplicated.

One can appreciate this criticism more fully by viewing a list of additional just-cause reasons as they might be applied to a particular war. We can assume, for the sake of presenting these reasons, that it is clear who the aggressor is. We can also assume that this aggressor deliberately provokes the victim nation just short of providing a sufficient just-cause reason for war. The aggressor, as it were, teases the victim nation with a small harm here and there.

1. There is an 'accidental' ship sinking involving the loss of life. Within a month a second 'accidental' sinking occurs.
2. Missiles are fired near the 'victim nation's' shores. The firings are said to be tests of a new missile system.
3. Rockets are fired over the border on a regular basis. The rockets are not fired by regular military forces, but by rebel groups embedded in the nation on the other side of the border. Casualties are usually light but occasionally a rocket hits a population centre and kills a dozen or so people.
4. An explosion in space caused by a missile disables several civilian and military satellites.[2]
5. 'Viruses' cause significant damage to computer programs that run the nation's military and banking hardware.
6. Terrorists assassinate two key government officials who are living abroad.
7. Terrorists destroy a building. A few people are killed.
8. Mines are laid in high-density sea lanes.

The multiple-reasons process complicates the just cause principle in another way. It is not clear how one is supposed to 'add up' the various good reasons (or contributing just causes) so that they reach the status of one sufficient just cause. Does one join up the various good reasons 'intuitively'? If so, the process will likely be very chaotic.

The second complaint is that modifying Just War Theory obviously opens the door to so many new reasons for going to war that the theory no longer constrains war. It looks as if any nation or group can cobble together a bunch of reasons and go to war any time it pleases. Put differently, it looks as if the theory is no longer doing any work. It is, after all, supposed to be a constraining instrument. If it doesn't do that job very well, we might as well throw it into the dustbin.

REPLY

Dealing with the second complaint first, it must be admitted that the modified version of just cause is more permissive of war than the classic version. To be sure, even the classic version would be less permissive if, instead of allowing for six kinds of just cause, it allowed for only one or two. But although more permissive, the modified version is not totally permissive. It still forbids aggressive wars and also forbids starting wars because of sanctions, economic pressures and ideological reasons (e.g., for the sake of communism, Christianity, democracy). What it allows above and beyond the standard theory are wars triggered by a series of small acts of aggression, assassinations, sabotage, systematic harm done to a people (serious enough but short of a humanitarian disaster) and the like. It permits war when these kinds of reasons are cited in series rather than as one large just cause. So the modified version of just cause is more permissive, but not much more than might at first be supposed. This will be discussed in later chapters.

As to the first complaint, one might wonder why the just cause principle should be modified at all. Why not leave it alone to reflect the traditional roots of JWT? What gain is there in modifying a classic principle when it is admitted that the modified principle is more complicated and more permissive?

The answer comes in two steps. The first concerns the nature of theories as such. Theories are instruments or tools that help us to deal with complex problems. They take on the shape they do for a variety of reasons. With public theories such as Just War Theory, political and logical reasons get involved in the mixture. For example, in the west, JWT seems to be shaped so that it speaks to nations rather than to ethnic, racial or political entities below the level of nationhood. In this regard, the theory is shaped by the political views of its originators. If the views are keyed to national entities, then, understandably, a legitimate authority principle will appear in and be very important for the theory. Nations have official leaders and the principle of legitimate authority designates which of these leaders have the authority to start a just war. Other features of the theory, such as the proportionality principle, are there because of how we humans think (i.e., because of logical considerations).

However a theory develops, there is nothing in it that says its principles must be set in concrete. Just the opposite. As a tool for thinking, a theory needs to be changed if change helps get its assigned task done more efficiently. If a theory, or any part of it, has developed in a way that constricts our thinking, then it should be changed. So the first step in understanding why the just cause principle might need to be altered is to realize that there is nothing wrong or abnormal about change.

The second step focuses on the kind of change being proposed – a logical step. As already noted, the classic version of just cause encourages 'singular' thinking. It does not actually forbid thinking in terms of a series of just causes, but is usually stated in such a way that those who apply it tend not to think in such a way. That just cause could be a series of causes, instead of a massive single one, doesn't seem right to many of those who consider the ethics of war. This discussion of serial causes is intended as a corrective. It reminds us that our thinking about the ethics of war need not be rigidly tied to a pattern of decisionmaking that is not mirrored in choices we make in other realms of life. In these other realms – of personal, business and academic matters – we think singularly some of the time and serially at other times. We usually engage in singular thinking when what concerns us is a simple matter. 'Should I go to work early today? Yes, the report has to be ready for our departure to

Tokyo in the afternoon'. When the matter that concerns us is complex, singular thinking may still suffice. 'I am getting a divorce. After all, he was cheating on me even before we were married'. But complex matters tend to encourage serial thinking. 'I am getting a divorce because he is thoughtless, selfish, cruel at times, crude and I find that when he is around I am miserable. The children are miserable too'.

War is often like a complicated divorce, because international relations are themselves complicated. As a result, there may be many good reasons for going to war. If the theory one holds about the ethics of war prevents, or discourages, one from recognizing this fact, then it ought to be changed.

Still, there is the objection mentioned earlier that the theory tells us nothing about how we are to manage the numerous and disparate good reasons that the modified just cause principle offers us. Without help from the theory, it would seem that our thinking would be ruled by chaos.

In reply, it is not obvious that the *theory* needs to tell us anything about managing our rich collection of good reasons. We need help not from JWT, but from a broadly construed sense of logic. There are logical or rational ways of dealing with multiple good reasons when decisions need to be made. To appreciate this point, all we have to do is examine how we deal with multiple reasons in the domains of ethics other than war. On those (rare) occasions when we make rational decisions we normally do certain things.

1. We carefully list the reasons, making certain that we have not left any out.
2. We edit the reasons in order to eliminate any intemperate or propagandistic language found in them.
3. We gather facts to determine whether the reasons actually apply to the situation.
4. We identify some reasons as being more important than others.

5. We compare the weight or seriousness of the reasons with an important and known reason (e.g., border-crossing aggression).
6. We arrive at a tentative conclusion(s) about how to act.
7. (With an open mind) we discuss our reasoning processes and conclusion(s) with other rational and informed individuals.
8. We then review the whole process either alone or with a set of advisers.
9. Finally, we make a decision.

There is nothing sacred about this process of reasoning. Some may favour a somewhat different process. But steps like these help to bring order to chaos. Still, critics may object that these steps are too abstract to do much good. What is wanted, they say, is a calculus to get things exactly right.

What must be kept in mind, however, is that such a calculus exists neither in the other ethical realms nor in the prudential realm. In spite of that, they get along reasonably well. No one rejects these processes of practical reasoning because they are too abstract. People do what they can with what they have. The argument here, then, is that it is the same for war. What is good enough for all the other realms where we engage in practical thinking is good enough for war.

BACK TO IRAQ

Now to return to the war in Iraq. This discussion, as to how just cause is to be conceived, started within the framework of the more general discussion concerned with 'harder' cases. However, when that discussion turned to the Iraq War, it appeared that that war was not a good example of a harder case; it was too easy to argue that the war was unjust, especially with regard to the just cause principle: there was no single just cause. However, if the principle is modified, the issues surrounding the war become at least somewhat harder to deal with. It appears that way even without the 'good reason' most favoured by the neo-conservatives. That reason has to do with democracy. The desire to spread democracy throughout the world was probably the primary reason for war for the neo-conservatives – this may even have been a sufficient reason for war.

Be that as it may, even without the democracy good reason, there are probably enough good reasons on our list to tempt some people to think that the Iraq War was justified. For the rest of us, these reasons may not convince us but they may at least instil doubts about the justice of the invasion. In this sense, by modifying the just-cause principle, the Iraq War turns from an easy into a somewhat more difficult case.

At this point, the question returns: are we making progress? How can a more complicated version of a principle that creates problems for us be thought of as an improvement on an older version in dealing with a war like that in Iraq? In the case of that war, it can't count as an improvement if one's mind is made up that the war is immoral. Having settled on that conclusion, any further discussion looks like backsliding.

But that sort of argument begs the question. The modification to the just cause principle was made for logical reasons. The logical point is that there is a flaw in the reasoning process concerning the just cause principle. The flaw in the standard theory is that it demands, or encourages, 'singular' thinking. It is possible, then, that those who condemn the war arrived at their conclusion, in part, because of a piece of overly-narrow thinking. To avoid that trap, the just cause principle needs to be modified

Indeed, after it is modified, and after the modified version has been applied to the Iraq War, I would argue (still) that starting that war was unjust rather than just. But that argument needs to be made at another time and place. For now, the point is to come to appreciate the need for modifying the just cause principle. That need, to repeat, rests on the logic of decisionmaking and not on the views one happens to hold about Iraq or any other war.

In later chapters more will be said about the multiple-reasons change in the just-cause principle. In those later chapters, it will become clear that additional changes to Just War Theory are required. These changes, as we will see, are concerned not only with other principles in the theory, but with the very structure of the theory.

7 More Problems with Just War Theory

CUBA (IN THE 1950s)

Two cases will be discussed in this chapter. They will suggest that Just War Theory needs to be further modified in several ways. In contrast to the cases of symmetrical warfare discussed in earlier chapters, these cases deal with asymmetrical warfare where one side has great numerical and/or technological advantages over the other.

Fulgencio Batista was part of the 'Sergeants' Revolt' that ousted Carlos Manuel de Cespades' Cuban provisional government in 1933. Soon after, Batista became Army Chief of Staff, from which position he was able to control the president. Because of the unstable political scene at this time in Cuba, Batista found himself suppressing one revolt after another. He did so ruthlessly, frequently executing prisoners. In 1938 he was elected to the presidency. While in office, he championed reforms of various kinds that favoured the poor and disenfranchised, so when he left office in 1944, as the law mandated he should, he had come to be known as a ruthless leader but also as a progressive one.

Batista returned to power in 1952 as the result of a *coup d'état*. There was little resistance to his coup, even though people were fearful about what might happen. For a while, things went well. The Cuban economy thrived. Buildings, roads, bridges and schools were built, and the ever ready to rebel Communist party, among other parties, was willing to work within the government.[1] But the corruption found in previous administrations continued under Batista. Not surprisingly, unstable as Cuba was at that time, various opposition groups began to surface and some quickly turned to violence in their effort to overthrow Batista's regime.

One of the rebel groups on the scene was led by Fidel Castro. In opposing Batista, Castro at first tried to use his skills as a lawyer to make the claim that the Batista regime was not legitimate; it was, after all, the product of a coup. Having failed in this appeal, Castro turned to more violent means. At first he did not succeed. His most famous failure occurred when he and his group mounted an attack on the Mocada Barracks located near Santiago de Cuba on 26 July 1953.[2] Soon after the attack, he was captured. Later, in 1955, he was released. Upon his release, he travelled to Mexico and then to the USA to raise funds and regroup in order to make another attempt at overthrowing Batista. That attempt took place late in 1956 and it too was a disaster.[3] Castro and 82 members of what was now called the 26th of July Movement travelled in an overcrowded yacht named *Granma* to Cuba. Soon after landing, the group was ambushed by the Cuban army. When it was all over, no more than twenty managed to escape to the mountains.

The few who survived the *Granma* landing received help from other rebel groups but were soon able to survive on their own. In 1957 they gained strength. By then, the rebels numbered just under 1000. In 1958, after repelling attacks by the Batista forces, Castro, his 26th of July Movement and other allies began to go on the offensive. By the end of the year, the Batista forces began to disintegrate. Seeing how things were going, Batista fled Cuba, in spite of efforts by Castro to capture him. Castro took over the Cuban government in the first days of 1959.

In terms of Just War Theory, how justified was each side in acting as it did? Consider first just cause from Castro's point of view. He could not cite the traditional just cause reasons to explain his involvement in the war he was waging against Batista. Batista was not invading anyone so he and his government could not be accused of being aggressors. Nor could Castro cite the preemptive criterion since Batista was not threatening to invade anyone. He was not even acting in such a way as to create a humanitarian catastrophe. He was torturing and killing opponents of his regime who were unlucky enough to get caught, but it would be stretch of the meaning of 'humanitarian catastrophe' to so label these horrible events. To satisfy the just cause principle Castro would have to, and did, cite non-standard good reasons (just causes) similar to those discussed in the previous chapter. The good reasons he cited come down to four.

1. The Batista government is illegitimate since it was not elected by the people. Nor is it in place as the result of a revolution of the people. Instead, it came to power in a coup.
2. The Batista government is oppressive in that it executes or imprisons many of those who oppose it.
3. The government is corrupt. It takes money and resources for itself that could be better distributed to the people.
4. As part of this corruption, the Batista government has allowed itself to be manipulated by the US government and US business. It has turned Cuba into an economic colony of the USA.

It is not clear whether any one of these good reasons for triggering a revolution counts as a sufficient just cause for war. Perhaps number 2 does. But Castro used all of these arguments to build his case against Batista, suggesting that no one of them could fully justify the revolution, but all of them together could. And indeed they sound sufficiently robust to do the job; they are as robust as the reasons given to justify a wide variety of past and present revolutions. So it is probably correct to say that the 26th of July Movement and its allies had just cause on their side.

But what about Batista? Was just cause not on his side because the other side had already won that prize? Some would say that both sides in a war cannot be in possession of just cause. This is correct when one side is clearly identifiable as the aggressor. But in the Castro–Batista conflict there was no clearly identifiable aggressor. Castro was not an aggressor even though he and his people fought aggressively. He fought to liberate a land, not to occupy it. As for Batista, he acted to defend the government of Cuba, however corrupt it may or may not have been, against what he and his ministers viewed as aggression. So he too can be said to have acted in accord with the just cause principle.

Thus far, then, both sides can claim that they are on the side of the angels with respect to Just War Theory. So what about last resort? Did both sides satisfy that principle as well? In theory there is no reason why they could not. They could have negotiated their differences through the courts or through meetings with one another. However, once Batista took power for the second time in 1952, social unrest and armed resistance developed quickly. Thus if he were thinking in terms of Just War Theory (which most likely he was not), he could have said that the last resort principle was moot. He and his government were already on the defensive against various aggressors and thus it was fitting for them to respond militarily to defend their regime.

On the other side, the rebels could claim, if they were seriously thinking in terms of Just War Theory, that the autocratic Batista regime was dealing ruthlessly with the opposition and so they had no room to implement the last resort principle. Both sides, in other words, could claim that they had reached last resort.

Once again, it should be emphasized that in going through the just war principles as they apply to Cuba in the 1950s, the point is not so much to present the reader with an historical view of how the principles were actually employed by Batista, Castro and others, but to show how the principles could have been employed. Could they, one might wonder, be employed at all? Or could some principles be employed, but not others? Or could some or all of the principles be employed only after they had been modified in one way or another? So far, we have seen two principles giving us a view of the just cause principle modified in accordance with what was said in the previous chapter, and a view of the last resort principle modified not at all.

What about the other principles? What about legitimate authority? In spite of its status as a regime that came into being as the result of a coup, the Batista government had no trouble in satisfying the conditions of this principle. In sending Cuban troops into battle, the regime was acting legitimately. With all its blemishes, it was, after all, the recognized government of Cuba.

In contrast, the rebels had problems with the legitimacy principle. Even if they were viewed as the 'good guys' in the struggle with Batista, how could they have established their legitimacy? To some, the obvious answer is that they received it from the people: the people made the rebellion just.

That answer is too glib. Most rebel leaders claim to be fighting on behalf of the people and to have been chosen by the people to represent them. In Castro's case, he talked as if he were the chosen leader, the legitimate authority, from the very beginning of the revolution.[4] Yet at that time he was only one of several rebel leaders who made that claim. Actually, there was no leader who had legitimacy although, of course, there were leaders in the rebellion since each had a following of one sort or another.

In time, a rebellion can gradually become legitimate as it transforms itself from a loose association of fighters with a leader to fighters who are engaged in war on behalf of a newly formed government. This is what happened during the American Revolution. The same thing may have eventually happened to Castro and his 26th of July Movement. However, early on in his revolution, soon after debarking from *Granma*, Castro's claims to legitimacy sounded hollow. He did not gain legitimacy simply because he claimed he had it; it is not gained by self-proclamation.

But granting all that, Castro's rebellion was not illegitimate. It would have been illegitimate if there had been a legitimate authority on the rebel side and Castro acted on his own without that authority's blessing. But since there was no such authority, Castro can best be described as acting neither legitimately nor illegitimately. That is, the legitimate authority principle simply does not apply to Castro and his movement since they cannot satisfy it in principle.

What we have here is an asymmetry in the application of Just War Theory. In the standard theory, there is complete symmetry. Each side has to honour the just cause principle equally, the principle of discrimination equally and so on. But now it appears that one of the principles of Just War Theory works for one side but not for the other. A nation at war needs to satisfy the legitimate authority principle; but a rebel group need not. One side has to jump over a hurdle; the other does not.

It should be clear why this asymmetry is present. The legitimate authority principle is a nation-centred concept. Nations have laws in place, some of which tell the people who is in charge of matters concerned with war. When two nations go to war, there is usually no problem in determining whether the war was started by a legitimate authority or not. Often, however, there is a problem with rebel groups that as yet are not well organized enough to have laws in place.

What of the principle of likelihood of success? Recall that all the *jus ad bellum* principles are supposed to be applied as the war or struggle is about to begin. In part, these principles are there to guide those in charge concerning possible military action. Well, at the beginning of the struggle, Batista and his people had no problem in applying the success principle: they had a good number of troops, their enemies very few; they had lots of equipment and money, their enemies very little. So they, and anyone else familiar with the situation, could say that they had a better than even chance of prevailing in the coming struggle.

But the likelihood of success principle played out differently for the opposition forces. Near the beginning of the struggle, Castro and his people had very little going for them. They were perhaps more motivated than the Batista forces, but there is little else to suggest that they had success in their future. Instead, reason suggested that they should abandon their effort.

But that can't be right because then Just War Theory would be telling most, if not all, rebel groups that they are acting unjustly since their likelihood of success is so low. Rebellions would automatically be immoral even if just cause were gloriously on their side.

The trouble here is that the likelihood of success principle (like legitimate authority) is designed for nations. When nations contemplate going to war they can count the number of troops, tanks and planes they have in relation to their potential enemy. They can also assess the terrain they possess. Is it suitable for defence? and so on. Given these numbers and conditions, it is possible for leaders of nations to judge whether they have any reasonable likelihood of success in war. But many rebel groups cannot make such assessments. Or perhaps it is better to say that they can make assessments about the hopelessness of their situation, but that these assessments should not count against the ethics of their efforts. Putting it differently, the likelihood of success principle does not apply to them any more than the legitimate authority principle does. It is a hurdle that they do not have to jump over.

Once again, then, but for a different reason, we come up against asymmetry. A nation must meet the principle of success, but rebel groups need not. So Castro and the other rebel leaders in Cuba during the 1950s were not going against Just War Theory by having little or no likelihood of success in their efforts to overthrow Batista. They were neither following nor violating this principle, simply because the principle does not apply to them.

Does applying the proportionality principle to Cuba lead to the same asymmetrical conclusion? To see whether it does, it is important to distinguish the proportionality from the success principle. Proportionality measurements have nothing to do with those concerned with likelihood of success. Rather, they are concerned with the good versus the bad that would come of war were it successful. So if Castro and the other revolutionaries could have pointed to the greater good (e.g., in the form of honest government, less suffering, more egalitarianism) that would be accomplished if their rebellion succeeded and also could have pointed to the lesser amount of projected harm that the rebellion would bring (e.g., in the form of only a few deaths), then they would have satisfied the proportionality principle. No doubt, the proportionality principle is difficult to apply. War is full of uncertainty and so, for example, casualties are often much larger than it was thought they would be. But it is not clear that this uncertainly applies more to rebellions than to many wars between nations. So it would seem that if nations are encouraged by Just War Theory to make measurements of proportionality in advance of the war's start, so should rebel groups. If Castro and the other rebels in Cuba had been inclined to think in JWT terms, then they could have made proportionality assessments about whether more good than harm was likely to result.

The problem with proportionality is not with Castro and his allies but with Batista and his. How were they to measure good (benefit) and harm? They could have done it, as they probably did, in terms of their own interests. They would then have chosen war if they thought that their interests would flourish, but not if not. But if they measured proportionality that way, they would not have been operating within the framework of Just War Theory. Instead, they would have been thinking like realists who say that ethics has no central place in war. According to this view, one might follow ethical principles in these matters but do so only if it suits one's self-interest.

If, instead, the Batista forces had thought in ethical terms, they would most likely have been acting against their own interests. After all, just about everyone except Batista and his group recognized his regime as corrupt. They could only enter a just war against the rebels if the purpose of the war was to win and be given time to bring about genuine reforms in the government. Such a purpose was, to be sure, remote. Still, reform is what Just War Theory would have asked Batista to try to bring about. Going to war for other purposes, such as to continue to control and profit from their corrupt practices, would have been condemned by the theory.

On the *jus ad bellum* side of JWT, the last principle in need of discussion is good intentions. Roughly what was said about proportionality applies to this principle. It is possible, without changing the theory, to imagine Batista satisfying it. His intentions would have been good had he fought the radical insurgents in order clear the way for reform. 'Yes', he could have thought to himself, 'my government is corrupt at present. But I mean to change it so that instead of serving ourselves we serve the people'. No one believes that Batista had such thoughts, but that is beside the point; the point, rather, is that these are the thoughts Just War Theory would have asked him to have, so it is in terms of these thoughts that we judge him. If, instead, his thoughts ran as follows then the theory condemns him: 'Yes we must fight Castro and all that rabble because if we do not, we will lose power and all the money that goes with it'.

Castro, his fellow rebels and his allies had no such difficulty acting with good intentions. They had good reasons for going to war against Batista. Presumably they acted, at least in part, to satisfy their good intentions; that is, they acted to correct the injustices (listed under the just cause principle) perpetrated by Batista and his people.

But what of the *jus in bello* principles? Proportionality poses no special problem in wars like that in Cuba. Rebel leaders can cause excessive harm to their own forces and those of their enemy either intentionally or because of miscalculation, but these sorts of disproportionalities are found in any war. In all wars one or more campaign or battle will violate the principle of proportionality – that is the nature of the beast.

In contrast, issues pertaining to discrimination are more difficult. The main problem is the greater willingness of rebel groups to make exceptions to the discrimination principle. Often, they argue that their desperate situation as underdogs leaves them with no recourse but to attack civilians, mistreat prisoners and, in general, be more brutal than they otherwise would like to be. Not to act that way is to doom their enterprise to failure.

In assessing arguments like this one, one cannot help but notice the high level of rhetoric (on both sides usually), and wonder just how convincing this rhetoric is in making exceptions to discrimination sound plausible. 'Our enemies are not just wrong; they are absolutely wrong. And we are not just right, we are completely and without question right'. With this kind of talk taking place, there is not much room for discussion.

But the main problem is that Just War Theory is not clear about how to deal with exceptions. There is a vagueness in the theory that allows different theory defenders to take different stances. Those theorists who follow the Principle of Double Effect (PDE) read the theory so that no exceptions are permitted within the discrimination principle. The PDE says simply that we cannot intend to harm innocents. Under certain conditions they may be harmed unintentionally, but not intentionally. Now the question becomes: who counts as innocent (civilian, etc.)? If prisoners are classed as innocent, then both sides in Cuba violated the principle of discrimination, even if their rhetoric made it sound as if they had not.

But many just war theorists do not accept the PDE. They argue that the discrimination principle is only a strong presumptive principle. This means that under certain (special) circumstances the principle can be overridden. One such circumstance would be where there is a clear choice between intentionally killing a few innocents or unintentionally killing many, many innocents. So there are two ways to read the discrimination principle. Some allow no exceptions to the intentional killing of innocents, while others allow a few exceptions.

But that is not the sort of argument with which rebels are concerned when they are faced with making exceptions to the discrimination principle. Their argument is that either they intentionally kill innocents or they lose the war. In effect, they pit the lives of innocents against their chosen 'cause'.

There are two things wrong with this way of thinking. First, given the rhetoric that follows in the train of a 'cause', it is easy to overvalue it. If our cause is successful, all the world's problems will evaporate and, forever more, people will be happy. The rhetoric fools not only the listener but the speaker as well. With an over-valued cause (or ideology) fixed in the brain, it then becomes relatively easy to undervalue the lives of others, including those who are innocent. Second, the logic of this either/or thinking is flawed. It isn't very often, if ever, that the choice is either to kill innocents or lose the war. What is true is that killing innocents is the most expedient option available to defend the cause: innocents usually make easy targets. It is also expedient because killing innocents is an effective way to fight wars. But in almost all situations it is just false to say that the choice is simply 'kill innocents or lose'. There are other ways to fight such as attacking military installations and personnel, attacking police and attacking certain high officials who are affiliated with the military and the police.

Given these considerations, it appears that to the extent that Castro's forces and those of other groups made exceptions to the discrimination principle, they were not justified in doing so. They evidently did not behave ruthlessly in all their engagements. Castro himself knew the rhetoric of 'good behaviour' and claimed repeatedly that his movement did all it could to avoid harming those who were not directly involved in the struggle to liberate Cuba from the Batista stranglehold. Still, at times there were lapses.

Of course, the Batista forces are subject to the same kind of criticism. They too made exceptions to the discrimination principle that they justified with even faultier arguments; they did not even have a 'cause' that they could use to justify their harsh behaviour.

AFGHANISTAN 2001

The case of Cuba above suggests that Just War Theory needs to be modified in several ways. First, the principle of legitimate authority has no work to do when certain rebel groups are involved in a war. Second, the same holds true for the principle of likelihood of success – it makes no sense to demand that rebel groups calculate a high level of success before they can be said to satisfy JWT. Finally, as the result of these changes, it appears that the theory needs at times to be applied asymmetrically. A further change was suggested in this and the previous chapter with the just cause principle. The change was characterized as 'logical' in nature. It allows a series of small just causes (good reasons) taken together to generate an overall just cause sufficient in strength to justify starting a war.

But so far, these changes are no more than suggestions. To help decide whether they should be accepted or rejected, we will look at another case. This is an interesting one for our purposes since it has to do with a war that is both symmetric and asymmetric.

The Afghanistan war was a direct outgrowth of the 9/11 attacks on the Twin Towers in New York, the attack on the Pentagon and the attempted attack on the White House. After the attacks, it didn't take the US government long to gather enough evidence that al Qaeda carried out these attacks.[5] Once al Qaeda was identified as the culprit, it seemed obvious that the US and a supporting cast of allies should respond somehow.

The problem, however, was that al Qaeda's main headquarters and training grounds were in Afghanistan, a country controlled at that time by the Taliban. The Taliban, an Islamic fundamentalist group, had invited al Qaeda as guests in their country after al Qaeda had been thrown out of its African base in the late 1990s. So if the response was to be an attack against al Qaeda, there also had to be an attack on the Taliban government.[6] There had to be two wars; one asymmetric and one symmetric.

Justifying the former in terms of Just War Theory was relatively easy. The USA certainly had just cause – it had been attacked and it was responding as soon as it could. Within a month or so, the USAF was destroying al Qaeda camps and facilities. Special forces were also present in the area engaged in 'spotting' for air attacks and supporting indigenous Afghan forces that were opposed to the Taliban. The only peculiar feature in this appeal to just cause was that the enemy was not a nation but a loose collection of fighters with no land of their own.

Such was not the case with the attacks on the Taliban government. It was in charge of almost all of Afghanistan with only the northeast corner being an exception. That land was controlled by groups of Uzbeks and Tajiks who together formed what was called the Northern Alliance. But appealing to just cause in order to attack the Afghan government was not as straightforward as with al Qaeda. After all, the Taliban government had not attacked the USA or anyone else. Weak as it was militarily, it was not about to attack any of its neighbours either. Further, the Taliban government was not churning up a humanitarian catastrophe within its borders. So the standard just-cause reasons were not available to the USA and its allies to justify going to war with the Taliban government.

The kind of justification needed would have to be an extension of the standard. The reason for that has to do with the peculiar relationship between al Qaeda and the Taliban. Allies are usually separated from one another geographically – one can be attacked without attacking the other. That was not possible with the al Qaeda/Taliban relationship, since the former was located inside Afghanistan. As an orphan, al Qaeda had been given a home in that country. From the American point of view, it would have been much the same if a neighbour had knowingly housed and supported a famous criminal gang. In short, the Taliban government was more than an ally; it was almost, if not quite, a co-conspirator. So because of al Qaeda's home inside Afghanistan and because the Taliban government had a very cosy relationship with the aggressor, it was deemed right that the Taliban government be attacked.

This extended sense of just cause might make some people a little nervous. But as was made clear in the previous chapter, the just cause principle can and should be extended; the standard conception is just too narrow and rigid to deal with all the contingencies of war. Besides, the USA nodded in the direction of last resort so as to make the war somewhat more acceptable. Instead of attacking immediately, it asked the Taliban government to hand over the al Qaeda suspects in their country to the USA. In effect, the Americans were saying 'give up the criminals and there will be no war'. But the Taliban refused to hand over their 'guests'. Soon after, the war in Afghanistan started.

Of course the 'war' thought of in international terms had already started with the 9/11 attacks. The immediate criticisms of al Qaeda had to do with the principles of discrimination and last resort. Innocent people had been attacked and attacked, it seems, as a first rather than a last resort. In fact, these were surprise attacks like Pearl Harbor and Port Arthur (in the Russo/Japanese War early in the twentieth century). Some criticism in terms of just cause was also present. But most of that was clearly heavily laced with ignorance: few in 2001 had any idea what reasons al Qaeda had for attacking the US. For this same reason, when they discussed 9/11 in proportionality (*ad bellum*) terms, their criticisms of al Qaeda were far off the mark.

However, little if any criticism was aimed at al Qaeda's failure to satisfy the legitimate authority principle. The explanation already offered for this failure is that, dimly perhaps, people realized that al Qaeda had no one in its organization who counted as a legitimate authority, so no one expected al Qaeda to satisfy that principle in 2001.

In one important sense, the same is true of the likelihood of success principle. Al Qaeda cannot satisfy that principle either. At first blush it seems otherwise. Al Qaeda could have, and probably did, calculate the likelihood of success of the 9/11 attacks. Their people planned the attacks carefully and knew that security arrangements at some airports and on many planes were not that good. So they probably thought that the success probability of the missions was high. Still, the likelihood of success principle is not concerned just with mission success; it speaks to the war as a whole. The principle tells us that war should not be entered into if there is a low probability of succeeding in that war. The point here, then, is that there is little to go on to tell al Qaeda or anyone else what the possibility of their overall success may be. We might all make guesses, but guesswork is all we have.

LOOKING BACK

This and the previous chapter are exploratory in nature. Case studies are used in these chapters to define the limits of Just War Theory, and limitations have apparently been uncovered. Just War Theory as it is classically understood appears to be too narrowly constructed. It is able to deal well with nation versus nation warfare. Even here, it has its limitations, especially with respect to the principle of just cause. That principle tends to encourage us to look for a single just cause, but there are times when more than one just cause (good reason) comes into play. But the main limitations of the theory become apparent when wars between a nation and a non-nation group are considered. Now at least two of the principles of classic Just War Theory look as if they need to be modified. The legitimate authority principle seems to have no application when non-nation groups (rebels, terrorists) are about to be involved in war. Similarly, the likelihood of success principle has no, or very little, application to non-nation groups.

Other changes in the principles might be in order. It is not yet clear, for example, whether the principle of discrimination should be changed. Should a weaker version of that principle be in place for the benefit of rebel groups and their causes? More exploration is needed here. More exploration is also needed to determine whether the overall structure of Just War Theory needs to be altered as a result of changes made to the individual principles. The next chapter continues that process of exploration.

8 Prevention: Sri Lanka, Thailand

ONCE AGAIN

There has already been some discussion of the distinction between preemption and prevention. In classic Just War Theory, specifically in the just cause portion, the former is allowed while the latter is not.[1] Preemptive strikes are allowed when there is a serious and imminent threat to a nation. In such a situation it is not deemed necessary to take the first, possibly fatal, blow. But with prevention, there is no first blow to take. The enemy is not ready to attack, nor will it be ready in the near future. So at this point the appeal is to the principle of last resort. Since there is time to prevent a future enemy attack there is no need to attack now, but there is time to take steps in order to deter a distant future attack, and to negotiate. In effect, as already noted, this means that even if Iraq did have weapons of mass destruction in 2003, Just War Theory does not countenance starting a war. It means that Israel's attack in 1981 on Iraq's nuclear facilities is also not countenanced. Nor is Germany's attack on Russia in 1941 and Japan's attack at Pearl Harbor in 1941.

All that is reasonably clear. Admittedly, there is a problem of vagueness with the preemption and prevention concepts. Is an attack preemptive if the enemy attack is known to be scheduled one week from now rather than tomorrow morning? What about two weeks? Very likely the answer to these questions depends on what the victim nation can do in the meantime. If the attack was in a week, and the victim nation could do nothing in the meantime to mitigate its effects, then the anticipatory attack would still be preemptive. But this sort of vagueness represents a small problem, since these sorts of situations are not likely to occur very often. It is not likely that a nation will have good enough intelligence to know where and when an aggressor nation is going to attack, and also not be in position to take steps short of war to blunt or prevent that attack.

Usually, then, the preemptive/preventive distinction is clear enough when two or more nations are approaching war. But that is not the case when dealing with a potential war or conflict between a nation and some non-nation group. However, to appreciate fully why this is so requires investigating what struggles between these two kinds of political entity look like.

SRI LANKA

Consider the scenario in Sri Lanka. The struggle there is between the majority Sinhalese, who are Buddhist, and the Tamils, who are mostly Hindu. There are also language and cultural differences separating the two peoples. Trouble between them began soon after Sri Lanka (formerly Ceylon) gained independence from Great Britain after World War II. The situation gradually worsened. It got still worse when, in 1956, the Sri Lankan government passed the Sinhala Only Act.[2] This Act made Sinhala the official language of the country and generally favoured the Sinhalese over the Tamils in school admissions and government jobs. In the minds of some, this law corrected a bias against the Sinhalese. During the colonial days, it was said that the British favoured the Tamils. Needless to say, the Tamils looked at the new law in a different light and saw it as an act of discrimination against them.

Other events followed that alienated the Tamils from the Sinhalese dominated government even more. In 1972, the nation's constitution was changed so as to give Buddhism 'the foremost place' in government and society. Then in 1976 the Tamils formed a coalition party whose aim was to gain representation in parliament for the 1977 elections. The party, called the Tamil United Liberation Front (TULF), did well in the elections.[3] But because the TULF advocated cessation from Sri Lanka, it was banned. Adding insult to injury, the government encouraged the expropriation of Tamil lands by the Sinhalese.

Understandably, discontent among the Tamils increased. Talks between the two sides to settle their differences made little progress. Nor did passive resistance against the government's discrimination policies accomplish much. Soon, scattered acts of violence occurred, gradually increasing in number. But two events were especially crucial. The first was an attack on an army post in 1983 by a group calling itself the Liberation Tigers of Tamil Eelam (LTTE). The attack killed thirteen soldiers. In response, riots broke out in July of that year in the capital city of Colombo and in other areas. The riots led to the death of more than 1000 Tamils. Following the Black July Pogrom, as it was called, each side perpetrated a wide variety of atrocities against the other side's civilians.

But that was not the end of it. In 1987 the Black Tigers, a radical Tamil group, introduced the notion of suicide bombers into the struggle. The first bomber, a Captain Miller, killed himself and 40 Sinhalese soldiers by driving a truck full of explosives into an army camp. Evidently the captain and the Black Tigers were inspired by the well publicized 1983 Hezbollah attack of US marine barracks in Lebanon. Of the scores of suicide attacks that followed, one of the most famous was against the Central Bank of Colombo in January 1996; that attack killed 90 and injured over 1400.

Matters became more complicated when the Indian government entered the scene in the early 1980s with a peacekeeping force. The intent of the Indians was to broker some sort of peace agreement. They failed in this effort and, in 1990, they were forced to leave after angering both sides in the conflict. One negative after-effect of the occupation was the 1991 assassination of the former Indian Prime Minister Rajiv Ghandi by a female suicide bomber.

After the Indians left, there were more efforts to settle the dispute. These efforts took place in the 1990s and continued into the new century. The level of violence tended to wane as a result of these efforts; this is what happened in 2002. But in time, one side accused the other of cheating on the agreement and so the fighting resumed. By 2005, and into 2006, the fighting had turned into 'a full scale clash'.[4] The clash involved not only ground war but also bombing raids by the government and LTTE-sponsored bombs going off in Colombo.[5]

Well, what roles do the concepts of preemption and prevention play in the conflict between the Tamils and the Sinhala? Do they play different roles here than they do in conventional wars?

Consider preemption first. This concept plays only a minor role in this conflict. In the beginning, discontent triggered a series of acts of violence by various loosely structured Tamil groups. It wasn't as if there existed a well-formed group tied to an intelligence organization that told the Tamils they were about to be attacked. It is possible that once the struggle began, one or another of the attacks carried out by LTTE was preemptive; some 'mole' within the Sinhala military could have warned the Tamils about an impending attack. The same point applies in the other direction. But it is not likely that Sinhalese intelligence was so good that they could have anticipated the beginning of a struggle focused around a variety of small and isolated rebel groups including the LTTE. But, once the struggle was underway, they too would have acted preemptively if they had placed a 'mole' in the midst of one of the important rebel groups.

Still, whether or not the possibility of preemptive strikes existed, there is no distinctive moral issue at play here. A preemptive attack in a struggle like that between the Tamils and the Sinhalese is much the same as it is in a war between nations. For both sides, preemption would be allowed ethically, both at the beginning and during the struggle.

Ethically, what is of more interest is the concept of prevention. If starting a war according to JWT between nations by a preventive action is wrong, it seems that it must also be wrong in the Sri Lankan struggle. However, like preemption, it is not likely that the Tamils struck first in order to prevent a future attack by the Sinhalese. Rather, they struck because they felt frustrated at the lack of political progress. They wanted more autonomy; the Sinhalese did not want to give it to them. They wanted the Sinhalese encroachment on their land to stop; the Sinhalese did not want it to stop. The Tamils, then, may (or may not) be blamed for starting the struggle that cost so many lives, but they cannot be blamed for starting a preventive struggle.

Once the struggle was underway, however, preventive attacks probably became quite common. An attack aimed at Sinhalese military barracks can be thought of as preventive. If such an attack were successful in killing many soldiers and capturing guns and ammunition, it likely prevents the survivors from attacking the Tamils in the future. Or, if it does not actually prevent a future attack, it weakens or delays that attack. It is the same in a war between two nations. Any attack on the enemy's military establishment is going to prevent it, at least to some extent, from mounting an attack in the future.

But there is one difference. When nations fight each other they are in what we call a *state* of war. That means that they are disposed to fight at any time even if at any one moment nothing much is happening militarily. If during war one participant breaks the lull in the fighting by surprising the enemy, it does nothing wrong. But a Tamil/Sinhalese type struggle is more of an off-and-on affair than is a conventional war. No doubt, there were times when intense fighting took place in Sri Lanka not unlike that typical of wars between nations. At other times, the fighting was more guerrilla style with the Tamils attacking and then disappearing from the scene of battle. These attacks could be, and often were, very sporadic. At other times, there might be no fighting as such, but there would be a suicide attack on civilians. Still at other times, usually after some sort of peace agreement or truce had been brokered, there would be very little going on.

The question then is: how are we to think of this struggle? If after a peace agreement has been signed, the Tamils start fighting again, are they continuing the old struggle or starting a new one? The same, of course, can be said of the Sinhalese if they start fighting again. The honest answer must be that it is not clear what to say here. This is especially so when dealing with non-state groups, not all of which might have signed a peace agreement. But even those groups that have signed might think of new attacks as a resumption of the old struggle rather than a new one. They would probably think this way if there were signs that the Sinhalese were making serious efforts to improve their military capability during a lull in the fighting. If, however, the peace agreement had lasted for months or a year or so, then perhaps a resumption in fighting might seem like a new struggle rather than a continuation of the old. The same could be said of an extended lull. Some might think that new fighting meant a new struggle. Others might talk in terms of a new stage in an old war.

This ambiguity is typical of such struggles, yet quite atypical of conventional wars. But if the talk turns increasingly to new-struggle thinking, preventive action becomes ethically suspect. This is because a new struggle requires new justification; it is like starting a new war. It must fall under the authority of a new *jus ad bellum* argument and, if it is a preventive act, it must count as going against Just War Theory. Preventive fighting does not count that way in an old struggle since it falls under the authority of *jus in bello*. As such, preventive fighting would be seen as a fully acceptable tactic in an ongoing struggle. There is nothing immoral about preventing your enemy's *next* attack; what is immoral is trying to prevent the *first* attack.

So the Tamils, the Sinhalese and others engaged in violent struggle are under greater moral pressure. Because their struggles start at one point and stop at another, assessing their preventive acts is more difficult than it is in the case of nations.

THAILAND

At this point it is helpful to turn to another example of a state versus non-state conflict to illustrate a different problem with the concept of prevention. This conflict is taking place today in Thailand. Geographically the main body of this country is to the north; it is bordered by Cambodia to the east, Laos to the north-east and Myanmar (Burma) to the west. To the south, the lands of both Thailand and Myanmar narrow to form two 'tails'. Thailand's tail stretches all the way to the south until it reaches Malaysia.

It is in this tail that the conflict is found. The majority of those living in the south are Muslims; ethnically they are Malays. Their language reflects their heritage. In contrast, the people living in the north are Thai and their religion is Buddhism.

For hundreds of years the people of the south were independent and powerful – they formed the state of Patani (or Pattani). But by the early twentieth century Thailand placed a weakened Patani under its authority. Eventually Patani, and the other states in the area, became officially part of Thailand. But the people in the south never fully accepted this. They resisted the Thai takeover almost from the beginning. They resisted Thai governmental policies that encouraged the suppression of the Patani culture.[6] However, starting in 2001, the level of resistance began to increase. By 2004, the increase was significant. Then by 2005 the frequency of insurgency attacks increased with almost two assassinations a day, 18.8 bombings a month, 12.8 arson attacks a month and a total of 43 raids and 45 ambushes for the year.[7]

It is not clear exactly who is responsible for all this violent activity. There is an overarching organization calling itself the United Front for the Independence of Patani that holds many of the rebels loosely together. One of the stronger groups operating within the United Front calls itself Pattani United Liberation Organization (PULO).[8] There are some other identifiable groups, but many are not identifiable. It is not even clear whether some of these groups are permanent or form up when the occasion arises.

If we assume, perhaps contrary to reality, that the Thai government is anxious to act in accordance with Just War Theory in dealing with these arming/armed rebel groups, are they permitted by the theory to act preventively? If it was clear that a group from a certain village was responsible a month ago for a raid on a nearby police station, then the preventive action of attacking the group would be justified. It would clearly be an attack within the framework of *jus in bello*. To attack under those circumstances is merely to continue a struggle that has already begun and, in so doing, help prevent the next attack.

But what is to be done with another group from a nearby village that is just forming up and so could not have participated in the police station attack? It would seem that attacking that group would be a case of a *jus ad bellum* preventive strike and thus a violation of one or more of the principles of Just War Theory.

In order to keep from violating these JWT principles, it would seem that the Thai government should initiate negotiations with the new rebel group. That is, they should appeal to the last resort principle. But should they? Here is a group, we are imagining, that is bent on harming the government and many innocent people. It hasn't done anything yet, but it will be initiating some sort of attack within a few weeks. It has already gathered weapons. It would attack now but it needs more weapons and time to develop its plan of action. Perhaps it can attack in six months or a year. This is also a group, let us assume, that does not know it is being watched by the government. But if the government begins negotiating, the group will realize that the government knows what it is up to. The likely result will be that it disappears into the jungle.

There may be times when the last resort principle has application when dealing with insurgencies. It certainly makes sense for the Thai government to negotiate with PULO or the United Front from time to time. But because the men from our imaginary armed group can slip away so easily, honouring the last resort principle seems pointless. As a result, one would probably not condemn the

Thai government if it acted against the group in a preventive way before it had a chance to disappear.

There are other differences between a nation versus a non-nation struggle, and a war between nations, leading to the same conclusion. One has been already mentioned: some non-nation groups are not easily identifiable. It is to their (defensive) advantage not to let their enemies know who they are. But the price they pay for gaining this status is that it makes their enemy's appeal to an early resort in order to keep from being harmed to excess by the violence aimed at them. And that appeal appears to be justified.

A second difference that often comes into play is that the non-nation groups often do not possess public property on bordered land. Deterrent practices work best when one's potential enemy has something to lose if a war starts. Your potential enemy's borders start here, and end over there. Inside the borders there are munitions factories that your bombers can reach. Given such a setting, you can threaten the enemy with total destruction if it refuses to negotiate. But nothing like this is possible when dealing with many non-nation groups they have nothing of value that you can target your bombs at. So the next-to-last and other resorts prior to the last one are not there. Or, if some resorts are still there, they are likely to be fewer in number.

Another difference does not actually apply to our forming-up group example, but does belong to many other nation versus non-nation conflicts. Many (almost all?) of these non-nation groups quickly come to the point of challenging the principle of discrimination. Hezbollah is a good example. They attack 'innocents' as a matter of course. They are doing this with more sophisticated weapons that are both concealed and increasingly powerful. In applying these technologies, they are merely making use of weapons that first became available to wealthy nations; these technologies have simply trickled down to the have-nots from the haves. They will continue to trickle down so more powerful area weapons will become available to non-nation groups in the foreseeable future.

> Hezbollah still possesses the most dangerous aspects of a shadowy terror network. It abides by no laws of war as it attacks civilians indiscriminately. Attacks on its positions carry a high risk of killing innocents. At the same time, it has attained military capabilities and other significant attributes of a nation-state. It holds territory and sits in the Lebanese government. It fields high-tech weapons and possesses the firepower to threaten the entire population of a regional superpower, or at least in the northern half of Israel.[9]

A sense of egalitarianism suggests that it is only fair that Hezbollah, and other groups (terrorist networks, etc.), have sophisticated weapons. Why arrange the world of war to favour the rich? But putting area weapons (mass destruction weapons) in the hands of non-nation groups is inherently more dangerous. When a nation uses a powerful area weapon delivered by a missile, its origin can be traced and retaliation can follow. But when many non-nation groups attack with an area weapon that kills thousands of people and destroys a good part of a city, authorship may be unknown and may even be unknowable.

But if, by a lucky break, a nation comes by information about a future serious area attack, one that will take place in a month or so, what is it supposed to do? Wait for the attack to start and then respond after the fact? It would seem to make more sense to authorize a preventive strike that takes advantage of the lucky break.

SUMMARY AND MORE

New changes in JWT seem to be in the offing, this time within the principles of just cause and last resort. The changes have to do with the concept of prevention. This concept can be applied with relative ease in conventional wars. In these wars we can usually tell the difference between a preventive strike before a war starts and one that occurs during the war. We can also distinguish between a preemptive strike occurring before or during the war. But there is a problem with non-conventional wars. Telling which is which is not so easy. Non-conventional wars start and stop so at times it is not clear whether the violence that occurred yesterday is an act of preemption or prevention. More importantly, if that latter, is it preventing the first or the next attack?

The reason for distinguishing between a first and a next attack is that they are judged differently on the moral scale. An attack that prevents the first attack goes against just war principles. One that prevents the next attack (in an ongoing struggle) does not. But because it is difficult to distinguish between the first or next preventive attack in a struggle between a nation and a non-nation group, it is more difficult to assess these attacks ethically. It is certainly more difficult than assessing the preventive attacks of nations when they are at war with one another.

There is another difficulty at play when the struggle involves certain kinds of terrorist groups. Unlike the local terrorist groups in Sri Lanka and Patani, the groups I have in mind are free-floating; they are not especially tied to a geographical home. Instead they practise their terrorist trade anywhere and everywhere. The difficulty is that it is not always clear in the event that such a group is intercepted by the authorities whether those authorities are acting preemptively or preventively. A case in point is the group of would-be terrorists from England who, in 2006, were intent on destroying a large number of airliners flying from England to the USA. According to one account, British officials acted preemptively by intercepting the group very close to the time that it planned to strike.[10] In contrast, the Americans, it is said, would have intercepted it earlier, making the interception more preventive in nature.

In dealing with groups such as these it may, in the end, make no important difference whether a nation acts quickly (and thus preventively) or at the last minute (and thus preemptively).[11] With these free-floating terrorists it seems that even if the preemptive/preventive distinction can be made, it is not worth making. Nations will intercept would-be and active terrorists whenever they can and not feel concerned about the ethics of what they are doing. And rightly so. Such terrorist groups are hard to find and easy to lose once found. They are also fond of surprise attacks on soft targets and, increasingly, fond of using powerful area weapons that create many victims. Finally, in many cases, they break laws prior to their attacks (e.g., by gathering illegal weapons) giving monitoring officials an excuse to short-circuit their plans.

Other non-nation groups need to be treated in much the same way as free-floating terrorists are. This means that JWT needs to be changed so as to allow nations to attack non-nation groups preventively at least in certain circumstances. The reason for this change is that non-nation groups are not easy to identify or locate, and certainly not easy to place sanctions upon. These non-nation groups are nowadays also capable of doing a great amount of damage.

This change introduces another kind of asymmetry into JWT. What nations do when they face each other prior to war is the same as before: preventive strikes before the war starts are forbidden; after the war starts they are permitted. In the case of struggles between nations and non-nation states, nations are not forbidden from acting preventively before the struggle starts. However, asymmetry is such that the non-nation groups in the struggle are forbidden to attack preventively in the same way since their enemy, a nation, is visibly open to attack and is available for negotiations.

9 Two Just War Theories

WARS AND STRUGGLES

In the previous chapters, the ability of Just War Theory as we know it to deal with the variety of violent struggles between peoples was questioned. In particular there seem to be problems with the theory's principles of just cause, last resort, legitimate authority and likelihood of success. There may also be problems with the discrimination principle but, as yet, that has not been fully explored.

Given these problems, it appears that Just War Theory needs to be modified. One way this could be done is simply by restating each of the principles in need of modification. Thus the just cause principle would tell us about the usual good reasons for going to war (all six of them including preemption) but also add a condition allowing nations to attack non-nation groups preventively under certain conditions. Similarly the legitimate authority principle would be supplemented with a condition stating that non-nation groups do not have to honour that principle under certain conditions. The other principles could be similarly modified.

One problem with this approach is complexity. The theory would be harder to understand, state and apply because some of the principles, when modified, would be extremely complicated. But the main problem lies elsewhere. Putting all the changes in Just War Theory into one form blurs the distinction between international wars, struggles between nations, and between nations and non-nation groups.

Notice how in an effort not to blur that distinction I have systematically been referring to international conflicts involving violence as *wars,* while referring to conflicts involving violence between nations and non-nation groups as *struggles.* Unfortunately the war versus struggle terminology has its downside. Some struggles are wars or very close to it. In these struggles, the killing and maiming is done in the same way and just as frequently as in international wars. So if the distinction between wars and struggles suggests that a sharp line exists between the two kinds of violent conflict, it misleads us. Still, nation versus non-nation struggles (or 'wars') that look like war are at one extreme. Non-nation groups occasionally fight as if they are at war. More often they engage in guerrilla war. Here we still use the term 'war' but with some misgivings. The misgivings are diminished when there is fighting practically every day; but when the fighting becomes sporadic we are less sure how to characterize what is happening. We are still less sure when the violence is primarily terrorist in nature. Some will still talk of war taking place as in 'the war on terrorism'. But some will simply be content to characterize terrorism as terrorism. Still others prefer to talk of terrorism as criminal behaviour and the effort to corral these terrorists as police work.

TWIN THEORIES – JWT-R

There is, then, no satisfactory term to cover the kinds of violent events that can take place between a nation and a non-nation group. Yet, these events differ enough from wars between nations to deserve being called by a different name. They also deserve to be treated differently; at least that is the suggestion I am going to make. The suggestion is that rather than try to pack all the changes mentioned above in Just War Theory into a super complicated modified theory, it is better to develop two versions of Just War Theory. One theory, what I will call Regular Just War Theory (JWT-R), will deal with the threat of war and actual wars between nations. This version deals with regular wars where there are two or more established national military forces facing one another. The other theory I will call Irregular Just War Theory (JWT-I). It deals with 'wars' (struggles, conflicts) between nations and non-nation groups.

It might be thought that there is something wrong with having two theories. Good theories are supposed to unify the domains of knowledge about which they are concerned. The model here is Isaac Newton's theory of motion.[1] Newton took the laws of terrestrial motion and those of celestial motion and combined them into one overarching single theory. So, the thought might be, rather than develop two separate theories about the ethics of war, a single overarching theory should be developed.

But notice a crucial difference between the overarching theory of motion Newton articulated and any proposed overarching theory concerned with war. Newton's theory combined two established and well developed domains of physics. There were known laws concerned with planetary motion that Kepler and others had given to science, and there were laws about motion on earth that Galileo and others had discovered. In contrast, no overarching theory about the ethics of war is possible for the simple reason that there are no two organized domains to bring together. We are blessed with having Just War Theory as we have come to know it (what I am calling JWT-R). But there is no twin theory to put alongside it as yet. Indeed, the purpose of this chapter is to develop and articulate such a theory. So even if it were eventually possible to develop an overarching theory about the ethics of war, violent struggle and all the rest, a separate theory from JWT-R would need first to be articulated. That is what I am trying to do.

So what would the two theories, each covering its own domain, look like? Regular Just War Theory is very similar to the theory that has come down to us by tradition. The following is a brief restatement (from Chapters 2 and 6) of that theory.

The first of the two-part theory is concerned with the conditions for starting or not starting a war (*jus ad bellum*). Recall that this part has six principles, all of which must be satisfied, before a war can be said to be just.

Just Cause

This principle generates six sub-principles. A nation can justly enter a war (1) if it is under attack now; (2) if it has been attacked recently and; (3) if it acts preemptively to head off a serious and imminent attack. The theory prohibits preventive attacks. But this principle also allows for entry in a war in order (4) to protect a friendly nation that is under attack now; (5) to protect a friendly nation that has been recently attacked and; (6) stop a humanitarian catastrophe. These are all sufficient causes; any one of them counts as a just cause by itself. Implied in how the list is presented is that it is complete. So other candidate just causes do not pass muster. Thus going to war for ideological reasons (e.g., in order to convert others to communism, democracy, Islam) is not allowed. However, going against this traditional way of formulating just cause, the principle was modified to allow for multiple reason giving (see Chapter 6). As modified, several reasons, each of which is not sufficient to count as a just cause, can be cited as a sufficient just cause for war. This modification complicates and weakens the principle to some extent. It complicates it because now there are a host of good reasons, not just six, that can play a role in the reasoning process to justify going to war. It weakens the principle because more reasons can justly lead nations to war. At the same time, the change puts the principle more in line with how we think when we make complicated decisions.

Last Resort

This principle is not to be taken literally since there is no way to identify war as the last resort. Put differently, the resort just before war does not carry the label 'next-to-last resort'. One can always slip in an additional resort between the one thought of as next to the last resort and last resort (war). Thus, instead of looking for a last resort, what is sought is a last reasonable resort.

So interpreted, the principle urges those who contemplate going to war to take a series of steps (e.g., negotiations, boycotts, sanctions, deadlines) before taking the plunge. How long the series should be is not made clear by the theory, so what counts as a last reasonable resort for one person is not necessarily the last reasonable resort for another. And what counts as the last reasonable resort for one war-threatening situation is not necessarily the last reasonable resort for another situation. In spite of this looseness, the principle still does important work within JWT since it can slow down the process of going to war. More than that, the principle may even prevent a war from starting since one of the resorts taken (e.g., negotiations) may be successful.

Likelihood of Success

A nation can enter a war justly only if it expects to achieve some sort of military gain. The nature of the gain will vary according to circumstances; it could be an outright victory or a successful defence. Even a partial defeat might satisfy this principle if the enemy has been stopped from achieving a complete victory. The principle forbids a nation to enter a war that promises nothing more than casualties. Famously, the principle is subject to manipulation. Leaders often cite a high level of success at the beginning of a war (e.g., total victory) only to settle for a lesser level after being exhausted by war.

Proportionality

If it is obvious that the benefits of going to war are far outweighed by the costs, then war is forbidden. Under this principle, one would not trigger a war to liberate a few thousand people on an island if that war promises to start a world conflagration. Because this principle suffers from a measurement problem (i.e., given the uncertainty of war, often it can't deliver credible assessments of risks and benefits), some doubt that it has much value in making assessments about the morality of war.

Right Intentions

This principle is usually taken to mean that a nation is acting in accord with just cause. Thus a nation has right intentions if it acts to undo some aggression or to undo an ongoing humanitarian catastrophe. Examples of wrong intentions are liberating a country and then annexing it, and invading a country in order to harvest its resources. Because of its subjective character, it is often difficult to determine what a leader's intentions are. The leader may know his/her intentions as the war starts but, often, most of us have to wait for later events to determine whether the war was started with good intentions or bad.

Legitimate Authority

Certain people or groups have the authority to start a war. These can be kings, dictators, legislators, etc. If others (e.g., ordinary citizens, mayors of cities) start a war, their war is said not to be authorized and therefore is unjust. The principle is not so clear as it was in the past. Presently, transnational organizations (e.g., the UN, NATO) claim to be legitimate authorities for certain wars. In these claims, they compete with nations for legitimacy.

The two principles that fall under the second (*jus in bello*) portion of Just War Theory are as follows.

Proportionality

Again, the expectation is that good will override bad, only now the overriding concerns are battles and campaigns rather than whole wars. If the harm is expected to be (far) greater than the good, then the battle should not be fought or be fought in some other way. It should be clear that a battle can be fought disproportionately in one of two ways. First, one side can apply *excessive* force and in so doing produce more harm than is necessary. But applying excessive force is not the same as applying *overwhelming* force. In certain circumstances, using an overwhelming force can save lives and so counts as satisfying the principle. But, second, a nation can act disproportionately by underwhelming an enemy; using too few troops can lead to disproportionate casualties for the underwhelming army.

Discrimination
Only certain people should be attacked intentionally. Soldiers, sailors, airmen, civilian truck drivers bringing ammunition to the front are among the legitimate targets. Those who should not be attacked include children, old people, mothers, secretaries, musicians, medical personnel and so on. Buildings and facilities also fall under the principle. Military airports, military barracks, submarine pens, bridges used to get troops to the front lines can be attacked, but religious institutions, hospitals and schools may not be. Often this principle is tailored to the situation by specifying Rules of Engagement that tell who should be attacked and how the attack should be carried out. The Rules may or may not specify how much collateral damage is to be countenanced. Also, the Rules may change as the war situation changes. The list of those places that might be attacked could expand if, for example, a building that was hitherto used for civilian purposes is now also being used as a lookout post. The list might also expand as the war becomes more desperate. So called dual-use targets might not have been on the list of targets when the war started, but may appear as the battle becomes more heated.

This, in brief, is the heart of Just War Theory-R. As presented it is unchanged except for the just cause principle that, altered, allows for multiple reason giving.

TWIN THEORIES – JWT-I

As presented, JWT-R serves as background to show how different Just War Theory-I is from it. The overarching difference is that parts of JWT-I are asymmetrical. In contrast to JWT-R, where each side is asked to play the war game by the same rules, parts of JWT-I allow for the two sides to play by different rules.

As with JWT-R, JWT-I divides into two parts. More often than not, both theories are concerned with events that last over a long period of time so that the rules for starting these events (*jus ad bellum*) are naturally separated from the rules for conducting them (*jus in bello*).

Just Cause

The nation involved in an irregular struggle (or 'war') follows the same six sub-conditions for regular war (e.g., can attack if attacked, etc.). However, it is now given some slack with respect to attacking preventively. The nation is permitted to attack a non-regular enemy that has not necessarily been clearly identified and may not even have been responsible for some not-so-recent attacks on it. If by chance or good intelligence it locates these irregular forces, it is allowed to attack them. Because of the great variation among the kinds of non-regulars a nation faces, the permission to attack preventively has to be granted on a case-by-case basis. In general, if the non-nation group has powerful area weapons, is in the process of collecting more weapons, is in the process of gaining new recruits to its cause and/or has plans for a future violent event, then it can be attacked. To repeat, it can be attacked even if it has not initiated any attacks as yet.

Nations are given even more slack when dealing with 'free-floating' terrorists. They do not have to be concerned with the preemptive/preventive distinction for various reasons. Primary among them is that terrorists can choose the time, place and the victims they can strike, and they can do so to a level of secrecy unavailable to larger groups and nations.

As to the irregular forces, they are permitted to initiate a struggle (or 'war') if the people they represent are being seriously exploited, subjugated, enslaved or slaughtered. They can also initiate a struggle when their 'brothers and sisters' (of the same religion or ethnic group in another nation) are being exploited. All these unhappy conditions that the irregular forces are permitted to react against can be thought of as forms of aggression.

However, one should be clear what the contrast is here. With JWT-R, the aggression usually concerns border crossings; with JWT-I, borders are usually not the issue. The aggression, if that is how it should be labelled, is usually internal to a nation – more akin to a civil war. The cause for which irregular groups propose to fight might also be characterized, with some trepidation, as stopping a humanitarian disaster.

Last Resort

Compared to last resort under JWT-R, this principle is, in one sense, defunct. The nation contemplating entering into a 'war' is not obligated to engage in the ritual of trying this and then that resort before fighting, because many of the resorts available in international settings (e.g., boycotts and sanctions) are simply not available when a nation is in basic disagreement with certain non-nation groups. Furthermore, the nation may not even know of the existence of rebel non-nation groups until the latter have already resorted to violence – it can hardly negotiate with entities that do not yet exist. But even if the non-nation groups exist, negotiations are difficult because the groups do not necessarily work together. Successful negotiations with one group may count for nothing with another group.

Yet, in another sense, the principle is not defunct. Although the nation may not know of the existence of all or some of the non-rebel groups until after they have struck, they most likely are familiar with political factions sympathetic to the rebels. These factions may or may not be in the nation's government. Either way, if they have grievances, these grievances can be negotiated. To be clear, these negotiations would not necessarily be with the rebel groups, which most likely have not even been formed during the (early) period of negotiations. Rather, the negotiations would be with those factions that happen to be articulating the social or religious group's grievances. Presumably, then, should the negotiations fail, the emerging struggle would probably be taken up by others who feel justified in creating rebel groups, who would say that the moderates have sold out. So there is a place for last resort in JWT-I, but it is a strange place. Often, a nation negotiates with one group (at least), but when the negotiations fail it fights with another group. Appealing to resorts before a struggle begins, then, is clearly different from wars falling under the auspices of JWT-R. In fighting under JWT-R a nation negotiates with and then, if things do not go well, fights the same nation; in fighting under JWT-I matters are much more complicated and difficult.

Like the nation approaching a 'war', rebel groups and their sympathizers need to honour a version of the last resort principle. They can do this, as the nation does, by entering into negotiations to settle their grievances. It would not do, if one wishes to follow JWT, simply to start suicide bombings, non-suicide terrorist attacks or guerrilla war out of the blue. It would also not do if the negotiations were perfunctory, thus giving the impression that some of the leaders of the aggrieved group are looking for a fight.

The negotiations are likely to be tenuous because of splintering – at best, rebel groups represent a loose coalition of the disaffected, with some unified sense of the direction of negotiations. At worst, as already noted, the groups will be splintered leaving the nation involved wondering whether an agreement they have made with one group will be honoured by another.

All these considerations leave last resort weakened overall. There will be times when a nation will not know with whom to negotiate and at other times that nation will not even know that it needs to negotiate. Yet there will be still other times when it will be possible to appeal to resorts short of the last one in order to prevent a conflict.

Thus honouring last resort will fall differently on the two sides. The rebel groups will probably carry the burden that they are the initiators of 'war', so they need to adhere to the last resort principle fairly closely; but the nation involved in impending 'war' will not carry the same burden. It will appeal to the principle in certain circumstances, but not in others.

Likelihood of Success

Applying the likelihood of success principle has always been difficult in war. Nations tend to overrate their likelihood, especially at the beginning of a war when they tend to overestimate their own military strengths and underrate their enemy's. The difficulty only gets worse when a nation deals with a non-nation group or groups whose leaders are largely unknown, whose military strength is unknown and who are located we know not where. Even so, if the nation has a fairly strong and stable military machine with at least an adequate intelligence organization, it has to calculate that it can apply the likelihood of success principle and from its perspective do so favourably. It may not be able completely to snuff out the rebel group so that it never comes back, but it can usually estimate that it has at least a fighting chance to suppress that group for a period of time so that the nation's economy and political structure will not suffer significantly.

Especially in its early stages when the non-nation group must decide actually to play the rebel role, applying the principle of success is difficult. It is not that it cannot apply the principle: it can. But, for the rebel group, the answer the principle yields is (almost) always negative. 'No', it tells the rebels, 'you have such puny resources that you have little or no likelihood of success. You will no doubt fail. So if you start a struggle you are acting against JWT'. However, that judgement is too harsh. It is one made with a principle that fits international (regular) wars, but not necessarily struggles between nations and non-nation groups. For JWT to condemn rebel groups for not satisfying the success principle is to invite them never to start their revolutions. No matter how just their cause might be, JWT tells them that they are acting unethically because they have little or no chance of success in starting their struggle.

The harshness of this principle means that it should not be applied to non-nation groups. We have asymmetry here. Nations must be asked to try to satisfy this principle, but non-nation groups are not required to do so by JWT-I.

Proportionality

There is no asymmetry here: both sides need to apply this principle, each in its own way. The nation can claim, for example, that the costs of going to 'war' with the rebels are likely to be less than the gain of sustaining their market economy. In contrast, the rebels can claim that achieving their political or religious goals is worth the cost of 'war'. In short, each appeals to its ideology and can see itself as satisfying the proportionality principle.

Right Intentions

There are no special problems with this principle: both sides can, if they decide to do so, act in accordance with it. Indeed, JWT-I insists that they do so. However, all the problems inherent in JWT-R (e.g., subjectivity) are found in JWT-I.

Legitimate Authority

Asymmetry returns once again. The nation involved in a struggle with a non-nation group must satisfy this principle. Each nation designates the individuals or organizations that are authorized to make war. All JWT-I asks is that they use these authorities when they are supposed to do so, but, typically, non-nation groups do not have legitimate authorities in their midst. They have leaders, perhaps charismatic ones, but these leaders do not have legitimate authority. Since they are unable to satisfy this principle, even in theory, JWT-I does not ask them to do so.

The following is an account of the *jus in bello* portion of JWT-I.

Proportionality

This principle works the same way in JWT-I as it does for JWT-R. So there is no reason why both sides should not make efforts to satisfy this principle.

Discrimination

The discrimination principle limits the exceptions we allow in war to the 'do not kill', 'do not harm', etc. rules in ethics. The principle tells us that certain people can be attacked but others cannot. However, in a struggle falling under JWT-I, national military forces face certain obvious difficulties: they often cannot identify their enemies; the rebels hide in rural and/or urban areas and do not wear uniforms; they look like innocent civilians; they often choose to fight in places where real innocents are found in large numbers. These difficulties make it impossible for the national forces to honour the discrimination principle to a high standard. This does not mean that they can attack innocents intentionally, but it does mean that the amount of collateral damage allowed by the Rules of Engagement will be greater – inevitably so. The choice is either to allow more such damage or demand that nations simply not resist rebel groups and, in effect, let these groups win because they have placed themselves in the midst of the general population.

The rebel forces do not have the same excuse when they attack civilians (innocents, those not participating in the struggle, etc.). They do not have the problem of being unable to identify and locate their enemy's military. Nor do they have the problem of separating their enemy from the general population. After all, their enemy is in uniform and is normally housed separately from the general population.

Yet, even though it is easier for them to follow the principle of discrimination, rebel (non-nation) groups regularly violate the principle. As noted in Chapter 7, they do so because they have become enamoured of the rhetoric of their religious and/or political cause. That rhetoric encourages them to narrow the range of those who count as innocents. At first enemy military and police personnel fall outside the circle of the innocent. Then the circle is narrowed to exclude those who profit from the enemy's political policies (e.g., civilians who move into lands the rebels claim as their own). Then it is narrowed further to exclude all adults who belong to the ethnic (racial) group of the enemy. Eventually about the only innocents left are small children and perhaps political prisoners of the enemy who are sympathetic to the rebel cause.

Put this way it becomes apparent how complete is the discounting of those who are normally thought of as innocent. In effect the rebel argument is that those who are even remotely associated or touched by the enemy military should count as combatants and are thus subject to attack. But such an argument is fairly arbitrary: it narrows the meaning of 'innocent' radically for no good reason. It is as if the narrowing of meaning takes place in order to make palatable the killing and maiming of those whom the rebels have chosen to kill and maim.

It is at this point that the rebel groups turn to a second argument to justify how they treat those that almost everyone else calls innocents. They say that they attack these people not out of choice, but out of necessity. Their weakness forces them to attack 'innocents'. But this is not as strong an argument as the rebels suppose it is (see Chapter 7). Aside from having the advantage in being able to locate their enemy's military (and themselves not be easily located), they have the advantage of being able to strike when they please. Their enemy's facilities, as it were, sit there in the open ready to be targeted. If, then, the rebels plan their attack, they are in a position to do serious damage to further their cause. They do not have to resort to attacking 'soft' civilian targets to get the job done. No doubt attacking civilian targets is easier, and it might actually be that better long term results can be achieved by hitting these 'soft' targets. Nonetheless, even if this point is granted (which it need not be), it does not follow that attacking soft targets is a necessity. Nothing forces the rebels to attack these targets out of necessity.

It appears then that the rebels can be held strictly accountable to the principle of discrimination. The standard they need to meet to follow that principle is actually higher than the standard their enemies need to meet. Their enemies cannot achieve a high level of compliance no matter how hard they try, because of the way the rebels are fighting. But the rebels can achieve high-level compliance because their enemies are always ready to be targeted.

Having laid out the dual versions of JWT in general terms, I turn in the next two chapters to criticisms of both the overall theory and the twin version of the theory. In the process, certain details of JWT will emerge that have so far not been discussed but need to be.

10 Problems with Just War Theory I

REALIST CRITICISM

There are problems with Just War Theory just as there are with any theory. Some of these problems were raised in Chapter 3. One of them was addressed in some detail; but the rest were put aside for later discussion. It is time now to look at these problems once again and to look at some new ones that have arisen from how Just War Theory has been characterized in this study. The discussion will move from an examination of the most general problems facing the theory to one that faces the particular version being presented in this study. That new problem will be discussed in the next chapter along with yet another new problem.

The issue discussed at some length in Chapter 3 has to do with how often JWT is used. The claim, remember, is that the theory is not used very often and so is not very important. The response to that claim was that the theory is in fact used more than is commonly supposed. Even if it is not clear how often it is used by government leaders who are authorized to lead a nation into war, others make great use of it. Politicians, lawyers, journalists, academics, religious leaders and even informed citizens look at decisions pertaining to war and assess these decisions in terms of Just War Theory. They engage in this assessment both prospectively and retrospectively. Prospectively – especially in democratic societies – they all discuss the issues that take a nation to the brink of war. These discussions are often vocal and public. Retrospectively, they hash over how and why a nation entered the war and how it fought it. The cases highlighted in the two chapters that followed Chapter 3 show how retrospective analysis works and how the wars looked at in those chapters have been extensively examined by followers of Just War Theory.

But even if JWT were generally not used as a way of assessing the ethics of war, that fact alone would not necessarily count as a criticism of the theory. After all, the theory could be ignored not because it is flawed in some way, but because it is not properly understood or promulgated. So even if it was ignored by all those who think carefully about war, that fact alone does not point to an inherent problem with JWT. Flaws in the theory itself need to be cited to help explain why it might be that the theory does not get more attention than it does.

The realists, already cited in Chapter 3, attempt to find a flaw. Actually, they claim to find several. One is that JWT is ignored as much as it is because of human psychology. We humans are built to look after our own interests.[1] It may be that on occasion we overreact emotionally and, as a result, act benevolently. But more often than not, when it really counts, we hew to the self-interest line in our actions. Thus, the problem with JWT is that it asks those who speak for their nations to act in ways unnatural for them. The theory tells these leaders to think about such important matters as war in idealistic – that is, unrealistic – ways. In part, then, the theory's insistence that people and nations act in ways that they are not inclined to act explains why the theory is ignored to the extent that it is.

But for the realist, JWT is not only largely ignored, it *ought* to be ignored. Idealistic wars, those that the realist supposes are supported by JWT, get nations into trouble. The 2003 Iraq War is a case in point. The American and British forces poured into that country supposing all along that the job of democratizing Iraq could be done quickly and cheaply.[2] It would be over in a few days and would be paid for by Iraqi oil. It didn't turn out that way. Optimistic assessments of how things might go were fuelled largely by the goal of overthrowing a tyrant and doing good for the world. It would have been better, the realists argue, had both the Americans and the British thought in terms of self-interest. Had they done so, they probably would never have invaded Iraq.

Working back in time, much the same could be said about NATO's involvement in Kosovo and before that the involvement of the UN, the USA and other nations in Bosnia.

Of course, it is possible that the JWT message coincides with the realist message. In Kosovo, for instance, JWT told the members of NATO that they should come to the aid of the Muslim Kosovars. The theory said that it was the humanitarian thing to do. Some realists might have recommended saving the Kosovars as well, but they would have made that recommendation not on humanitarian grounds, but on reasons related to the interests of the NATO nations. Unless the Kosovars were helped, Europe might become unstable politically.[3] Thus, the realists would have no objections to acting *in accordance with* JWT. That means that the realists are acting, for self-interest reasons, in parallel with just war theorists; but what the realists say should not be done is *follow* JWT. To follow that theory is to be led by its principles. That is what gets nations into trouble. More often than not, realists tell us, to follow JWT is to be led by the nose into disaster.[4]

Disaster stalks JWT in another way. It is bad enough to follow that theory *into* war; it is just as bad or worse to follow it *in* war. Again, JWT and realism might lead a nation to fight a war in the same way. Both theories might say, for example, that after a battle is over, prisoners should be well treated. The former would say this because of humanitarian reasons – there is no point in creating needless suffering; the latter would say that doing so is in the nation's self-interest. The prisoners might, if treated well, cooperate and provide valuable information to their captors that would otherwise be unavailable. Besides, good treatment of prisoners might also encourage the enemy to treat one's own imprisoned soldiers well. But realists would insist that when it is in the nation's self-interest to harm prisoners (e.g., perhaps when the enemy holds no prisoners), then it should not hesitate to do so. A nation is more likely to win the war if it acts on realist principles than on 'idealistic' just war principles.

The extent to which JWT harms the nation at war goes beyond how prisoners are treated. For realists, fighting a war by following JWT principles is like a person fighting an opponent with one hand tied behind his back. If you fight by the rules, but your opponent does not, he has the advantage and will most likely win.

But matters are worse than that. If those not following JWT know that their opponents are following that theory, and thus are acting unselfishly, they can take advantage. JWT tells its followers that they should not attack non-combatants. Knowing that, the enemy will mingle their forces with non-combatants.[5] When they see enemy fighters among the non-combatants, followers of JWT will hesitate before shooting, or they will not shoot at all. But their opponents will not be similarly restrained. JWT followers will most likely not lose if their forces are overwhelmingly large, but if the battle is a close call, everyone realizes that the followers of JWT will probably lose. The realist message is that if you aren't selfish, you won't survive.

What can be said about these realist arguments? In its extreme form the first argument claims that we cannot act ethically because we are thoroughly selfish in our motivations. This is a difficult position to defend. Humans exhibit all sorts of behaviour that, on the face of it, belies this view. Mothers unselfishly care for their children, and children for their elderly parents; soldiers sacrifice their lives for their comrades; many give money for the poor or stop to help the victims of accidents, or give help willingly when a family loses everything in a house fire.

However, to make their point, realists do not have to be extremists. They can merely say that people and nations act benevolently, and thus follow the principles found of JWT, very reluctantly. It is more natural for them to act in a selfish way. No one has to convince a nation that it should participate in a war when it is under attack or if its vital interests are threatened. But if a humanitarian war is in the offing, nations balk. They delay, negotiate endlessly and resort to sabre-rattling. And even when they finally enter the war, they do so with stipulations that ensure that their casualties and their other costs will be minimal.[6] The way NATO dealt with the Kosovo crisis – confining itself to an air campaign – is a good example of this sort of reluctant benevolence.

So, following JWT as a way of acting ethically is not easy. Nations have to be reminded, cajoled, persuaded, bribed and even coerced into right action. If this is correct, the realists have in their hands a legitimate criticism of JWT. It is a theory not likely to be used as frequently and as consistently as its defenders would wish it to be.

But how damaging is this criticism? It is tempting to think of it as quite damaging. After all, if theories are tools that help us do our thinking, they are useful only when they are used – an unused tool is like having no tool at all. However, it should not be forgotten that JWT is not strictly speaking an unused tool. It may be underused and we might all agree that this is a shame. But, as we have seen, it is used more often than is commonly supposed. If political leaders who make decisions about war don't use it as often as we would like, other political leaders, religious leaders, academics and so on do. Further, if it is underused to a greater or lesser extent, it is not uniquely underused. It is not as if JWT is more underused than any other theory of ethics. All theories, systems, outlooks, etc., of ethics are underused, and for the same reasons as JWT. Acting ethically is burdensome. It also has to be taught, and taught gradually and thoroughly – it is a long and difficult process. But it makes no difference what the domain is: it is all the same for business, biomedical, legal, mass media, family, etc., ethics. So if it is a flaw for JWT that it is not used as often as we think it should be, then it is a flaw for all the other ethical domains as well.

The second realist criticism is that employing JWT leads to bad consequences. Things go better if nations act in accordance with their self-interest rather than some moral ideal. More specifically, the argument says that if nations follow their self-interest they are actually less likely to become involved in wars.[7] There are serious injustices in various parts of the world; if nations are moved to correct one then another of these injustices in accord with JWT, they will become involved in wars that they would not otherwise have fought. In effect, the argument says that JWT is not doing its duty: its role in our thinking is to restrain war, but rather than do that, the theory, through its idealism, encourages war.

The other side of this argument is that it places realists in a position to claim that they are the true restrainers of war. This suggests that behind this restraining role, the realists have their own theory about the rightness and wrongness of when to go to war and how to fight it once war begins. The theory is rarely if ever explicitly stated, but here is what it would look like if it were. We could name it the Self-Interest War Theory. Another name it could go by is the Prudential War Theory. Like JWT, it divides into two parts.

THE REALIST PROCESS FOR GOING TO WAR (OR THE PRUDENTIAL WAR THEORY)

Good reasons principle (alias just cause principle)

When fully stated this principle identifies the specific good reasons for going to war. All of the reasons are variations on self-interest or prudence. So a nation can enter a war when: 1) it is being attacked, 2) has been attacked recently, 3) when preemption is advisable (i.e., a serious and imminent threat presents itself), 4) when an ally is being attacked and this attack affects the nation's self-interest, 5) when an ally has been recently attacked and this attack affects the nation's self-interest. Notice that items 4 and 5 allow a nation to pick and choose when it will come to the aid of an ally. Notice also that the humanitarian good reason is not in this list as it is for JWT. Finally, notice that there is another good reason that belongs in the list: 6) A nation can enter a war if it is clear that it is in its self-interest to do so. This is a good reason that JWT cannot countenance as good, because it allows a nation to be an aggressor. But being an aggressor does not count automatically as 'bad' for realists, since they are not making moral assessments as such. By their lights, if aggression promises to pay off, then one would be a fool not to be an aggressor.

Last resort principle
Resorts other than war should be tried first since war often has unexpected and dangerous outcomes. It is in a nation's self-interest to explore these outcomes. As with Just War Theory, this principle should be read as last reasonable resort. As with JWT, this principle slows the process of going to war without necessarily stopping it.

Likelihood of success principle
It is not in a nation's self-interest to get involved in a war with little or no likelihood of success.

Proportionality principle
Concern with the nation's self-interest or prudence demands that benefit and cost analysis should determine when a nation goes to war. Realists can apply this principle more easily than can just war theorists because they are only concerned with self-interest considerations. In contrast, just war theorists have the more difficult task of taking everyone's interests into account and doing so with an eye on fairness.

Good intentions principle
A nation's intentions should match the good reasons it appeals to when it goes to war. So it is easy for realists to satisfy this principle: no one doubts a nation's good intentions when 'good intentions' means 'acting in the nation's self-interest'.

Legitimate authority principle
It is in a nation's self-interest to have a system in place for making decisions about war. More than likely, realists would reject handing over legitimacy to supra-national organizations such as the UN. After all, these organizations usually have interests in mind beyond those of the nation.

PROCESS FOR FIGHTING WAR

Proportionality principle
Cost-benefit analysis for battles and campaigns is required just as it is for the process of getting involved in a war. Costs, of course, means costs to the nation's self-interest and benefits means self-interest gain.

Discrimination principle
This principle is not needed. What discrimination the realist practices falls under the proportionality principle. Thus if some noncombatants ('innocents') were spared, that would be because of some self-interest reason (i.e., cost-benefit analysis concerned only with the nation). One such reason might be that public relations are improved by being kind to civilians; another that noncombatants are needed to help repair buildings after the fighting is over. A reason that would not show up on the list is that noncombatants have intrinsic worth (and so should not be attacked).

Given a theory something like the one sketched above, it is understandable that realists can think of their position as war-restraining. Each principle, as with JWT, acts as a hurdle that needs to be overcome both before and after war starts. Realists promote the superiority of their own vision because it leads to fewer wars than does JWT. Their theory does not lead nations into well intentioned but generally foolish humanitarian wars.

Just war theorists see things differently. They can grant the correctness of the realist claim that they start certain wars that the realists do not. They can also grant the realist claim that many of the humanitarian wars they sponsor are ill-executed and thus may do more harm than good. In this sense, the realist critique of JWT has some bite to it. But the bite does not cause quite so much bleeding as one might suppose. Viewing matters as they do, the just war theorists will point out that some (many?) wars are, in fact, humanitarian: they do stop slaughters, they do bring food to the hungry and they do give shelter to the homeless. It isn't necessarily the case that all these wars are ill-conceived and mismanaged.

More tellingly, just war theorists can point out that realists are not necessarily on the side of peace more often than they are. Realists champion certain wars that just war theorists oppose, foremost among them wars of self-interest. If the neighbouring nation has oil reserves that we need desperately then, if we think that the international community won't scream too loudly, we should grab their oil. So it isn't as if appealing to JWT brings about more wars than appealing to realist doctrine. Rather, each theory encourages its own kind of war. JWT champions wars inspired by ethical concerns, realism wars inspired by self-interest or prudence. In the end, which theory results in more – and more serious – wars is difficult to say. But what is clear is that realists cannot legitimately claim that they are more on the side of the angels than are the just war theorists.

ONE-HAND-TIED ARGUMENT

The third realist criticism of JWT has to do with the one-hand-tied-behind-one's-back argument. The claim is that JWT severely restricts how an army fights: if soldiers have the enemy in their sights but there are civilians in the area, the soldiers are not allowed to shoot and the enemy gets away. Too bad! The realists say that the military should be unrestrained to ensure victory, but JWT repeatedly ties up the military thereby lessening the chances of victory.

What can be said of that argument? Well, again, it appears that the realists are onto something. There is no doubt that in many battle settings the limits JWT places on a military puts it at a disadvantage. But just war theorists have a reply: 'Yes we are disadvantaged in the short run. But our military cannot fight a consistently dirty war and keep its morale high, also keeping the support of people at home. So in the long run, we do best to fight a clean war in accordance with JWT'. Realists have their riposte to this. 'The reason your people cannot fight a dirty war, as you call it, is just because they have been propagandized by all this stupid talk about ethics. If, instead, your people were taught the realist ideology you could do what you need to do to maximize your chances of winning and thereby maximize the satisfaction of your self-interest. It's a sign of weakness that you and your people cannot do what you need to do to win'.

It may not be quite fair to say that realists believe people have been propagandized into acting ethically. But if that is what some of them believe they are most likely misled. The commitment to acting ethically is structural. Western liberal societies are built on ideas of individual rights and respect. This commitment isn't tacked on by a series of propaganda campaigns. In war, this means that western societies find it difficult to become involved in a fight in which non-combatants are attacked indiscriminately, a difficulty they admittedly overcame in World War II in the guise of various bombing campaigns: they got into the habit of attacking cities in both Germany and Japan.

Things have lately changed, however, especially since the Vietnam War when television cameras appeared on the battlefield and it became almost impossible for western forces to fight 'dirty' wars. If any western army attacked non-combatants as a matter of policy, and did so on a regular basis, it would be quickly disgraced in the eyes of its own people. In losing the support of the people and the politicians behind them, it would inevitably lose the war.

In short, fighting a 'no holds barred' war is not an option for western nations. They must fight within the framework of something like the discrimination principle. If there are costs in fighting such a war because of the 'one hand is tied' argument, then they must be borne. And, indeed, there are such costs. The realists are right about that. But they are wrong in supposing that in the long run these costs severely harm those who defend JWT.

Realists are also wrong in supposing that modern democratic societies can order their military forces to fight a 'no holds barred' war. Their model of how wars should be fought is obsolete. It is no longer in the self-interest of nations to fight such wars. They might inaugurate a propaganda campaign to convince everyone that this sort of war is needed, but the campaign, although it might be partially successful, would run into the liberal bedrock of western societies. The realists would eventually realize that it is in the self-interest of their own societies not to fight a 'dirty' war but, instead, to honour the discrimination principle at least to some extent. Thus, on realist grounds, realists would be fighting a war not too different in kind from that being fought by the advocates of JWT.

In sum, realism has injured JWT but not mortally. Realism is right in claiming that JWT is underused, but this is a flaw of all ethical theories. It is not as if realism can single out JWT for special criticism with the underuse argument. Realism is also right in claiming that JWT encourages humanitarian wars, but this fact does not prove that realism is more pacific than JWT simply because realism encourages other kinds of wars. While JWT encourages humanitarian wars, realism encourages wars of self-interest. Finally, realism is right in claiming that JWT handicaps those societies that want to follow it. But the handicap is one from which western societies cannot escape. They are under pressure from their liberal instincts to act ethically in war and so to follow something like JWT. To some extent, that pressure works on the realist theory as well. For example, it would not be in the self-interest of a western nation to act against the discrimination principle in a gross fashion. This shows that realism and JWT are not as far apart as is sometimes supposed, and that some of the criticism of JWT coming from the realist tradition rubs off on that theory as well.

WINDOW DRESSING AND MORE

JWT can be said to be underused in a different way. Politicians and military leaders don't have to underuse the theory by ignoring it; they don't have to underuse it simply by appealing to another theory. They can appeal to JWT for public relations reasons, but then ignore it when the time comes to make decisions. Making such an appeal is almost too common. Hitler did it when he invaded Poland (see Chapter 4). He wasn't following or being guided by JWT in justifying his invasion: he justified what he did in terms of German self-interest. The Poles, he said, were threatening the Germans; recall that he showed everyone the dead Polish aggressors as evidence. They were conveniently found in German territory because, of course, the 'aggressors' were put there after Hitler had murdered them. The North Koreans also claimed that they were fighting a just war against an aggressor (see Chapter 4 again) when really they had started the war in order to unify Korea on their own terms. The pattern is always the same: use JWT as a cover when you, as a national leader, are doing something contrary to what the theory tells your nation to do.

Critics of JWT jump in at this point. Some will be realists who will say that this is more evidence of underuse. But, more of them are likely to be pacifists.[8] Fitting in with their ideology, here is what they could say: 'We oppose JWT. Everyone knows that. We do so because the theory makes war acceptable. It encourages people to think that murdering your fellow humans is acceptable under certain conditions. JWT may even be interpreted as telling us that it is our duty to kill. Thus, rather than discouraging war, it does the opposite: it actually encourages war. But, in addition, we now see how many who do not support the theory use it to cover up their murderous ways. Used as a cover-up, the theory contributes to starting wars in still another way'.

Again, the critics have a point. There is no doubt that many nations have appealed to JWT, or theories closely affiliated with it, more as window dressing than as a tool for helping them make decisions about war. But one has to wonder whether the fault here lies with the theory. If a theory, any theory, is a tool, then there is nothing to prevent anyone from misusing it. The hammer is useful for building homes, but it can also be used for breaking into homes. In this vein, a just war theorist can use the realist self-interest theory as window dressing. She can appeal to realist reasons because she knows that, although she is moved by JWT, many of her people are not. In the same vein, she can use pacifist theory as window dressing with those of her people who are inclined to be sympathetic to that position. Once again, then, (almost) any theory can be used as window dressing for another theory, so JWT is not harmed by the window dressing argument any more than other theories. The argument does not point to a special weakness of JWT.

Still, the window dressing argument can be pushed a little harder. Granted, the critic may say, all theories are subject to this argument, but isn't JWT the foil in this argument more so than are other theories? It may be. War being such an important public activity, it needs an effective cover when there is wrong doing. What better cover can there be than one based on ethical principles?

But so what? Far from counting as a criticism of JWT, the argument can be turned around to enhance the status of the theory. Why did Hitler and Kim Il Sung use JWT as window dressing? Why didn't they use another kind of window dressing? The obvious answer is that they sensed that others, many others, are influenced by JWT. They wanted others, who were thinking in JWT terms, to treat them as victims rather than aggressors; that is, they invoked the theory (as window dressing) because they realized how influential it is.

The status of the theory is enhanced in another way by these abuses. When Hitler and Kim attempted to cover their aggressions by appealing to JWT, they indirectly committed themselves to the theory: the Poles and the South Koreans, they said, are aggressors and aggression is bad. If later it is shown that they were the true aggressors, they are condemned by their own words. In this strange way the theory is seen here as working even while it is being abused.

PACIFISM AGAIN

The above paraphrase of the pacifist position contains an argument in addition to the one concerned with window dressing. That argument claims that JWT rhetoric makes war more palatable and therefore actually encourages war. JWT thus does the opposite of what it says it does: instead of restraining war, it makes it happen.

Part of the difficulty of dealing with this argument is that what it claims is so sweeping. How do pacifists know that the language of JWT encourages war? It isn't enough for them to point to the vocabulary of JWT when it speaks of war. Expressions such as 'just war', 'just cause', 'legitimate authority', and even 'discrimination' may sooth the conscience of many warmakers. But when one looks not just at the vocabulary but instead focuses on the claims found within the theory, one gets a different reaction. Now we see JWT portraying war as something ugly; that is the point of having principles such as last resort in place. That principle tells us that war should be avoided because it is ugly, and to make sure that it is, we are asked to try this, this and that resort before going to war. A similar point applies to the just cause principle. That principle tells us that we must explain ourselves quite thoroughly before we can justly initiate a war. As has been noted many times in this book, each of the principles plays a restraining role. Far from viewing war in soothing terms the language of JWT, looked at as a whole, portrays war in darker, more disturbing colours.

11 Problems with Just War Theory II

LOOOSENESS

The problems with Just War Theory discussed in the previous chapter are manageable. That is certainly the case with the cluster of so-called underuse problems. The problem of window dressing turns out not to be serious at all; nor is the causes-war argument. But the problem of looseness is quite serious. It has its source in the loose way in which JWT is stated. Each of the principles, some more than others, suffers from vagueness, ambiguity or some other such fault so that different followers of the theory read each principle differently. In what follows I will comment briefly on each principle so that a sense of the looseness built into the theory can be fully appreciated.

AD BELLUM *PRINCIPLES*

Just Cause

Matters have been made worse by the change to the theory introduced in Chapter 6. Recall that the just cause principle was made more open-ended so that sometimes this principle can be satisfied with one overpowering reason and at other times with a cluster of reasons. The clustering causes more than its share of other problems. As explained, the theory does not tell us what reasons should be cited to make up the cluster. Nor does it tell us how to weigh the reasons. Even when logical considerations are introduced into the discussion, a considerable amount of looseness remains. But beyond that, the standard reasons (all six of them) generate their own problems. For example, aggression is usually thought of in terms of a massive hostile border crossing of troops. But then does a massive, or not so massive, rocket barrage count as aggression? What about an attack on a nation's weather, communications and 'spy' satellites? What if the satellite attack is selective so that some satellites are attacked but not others? What about an electronic attack that disables a nation's banking system? Is that 'aggression' serious enough to constitute a good reason (just cause) for going to war? The problem is that there are so many ways that a nation can be aggressive – it is impossible to draw a line between aggression on the one side and what is not aggression or not serious aggression on the other that most people can agree on.

Last Resort

This principle has always been troublesome. As previously noted, a literal meaning of last resort makes no sense. But even when this principle is modified so that it is read as 'last reasonable resort', the problems do not go away. What is reasonable to one JWT defender is not reasonable to another. The Gulf War of 1991 is a good example of the problem. Some members of the Democratic Party in the USA were chanting 'Give the sanctions a chance to work'. They were telling the first President Bush that there was at least one reasonable resort that hadn't been tried as yet. But Bush thought that the negotiations had gone far enough and that he had waited beyond what was reasonable for Saddam Hussein to respond.

Good (Right) Intentions

This principle also has always been troublesome. Unlike the vagueness found with the last resort principle, the problem now is mainly with subjectivity. Grotius complained about this problem to the point of banishing good intentions as a principle of JWT.[1]

The subjective nature of good intentions makes it at best difficult to assess a nation's intentions as a war is about to begin or even after it has started. More often than not, we have to wait until the war has been over for some time to see what was intended. But there is another problem with this principle. Intentions are complex. People and nations often intend more than one thing. In the Iraq War of 2003, the American intentions very likely included getting rid of Saddam Hussein, establishing a democratic regime in Iraq, spreading democracy to other Middle Eastern countries, helping the Iraqi people feed, clothe and house themselves, increasing the world's oil supply, increasing trade with Iraq, helping Israel and holding Iran in place. Identifying the good reasons in the list and then weighing them to determine if one or more is strong enough to serve as a good intention is no easy task.

Likelihood of Success

Ambiguity is a big problem with this principle. National and guerrilla leaders have a tendency to change the meaning of 'success' as the military and political situations change. One season success means 'total victory', the next, when things aren't going so well, it means something less. Of course, with this principle, there is also the problem of measuring the *likelihood* of success. War being the unpredictable creature it is, it is unclear that any objective measure of likelihood of success can be identified.

Proportionality

Measurement is a big problem here, too: very big. How could one have measured the good versus the bad of World War I in 1914? What about World War II? The Korean War? With these and other wars we can sense the heavy breathing of the pacifists. As we will shortly see, many claim that we can measure the costs and benefits of war and that the costs always override the benefits. At the beginning of war many don't appreciate this point. In their excitement, people tend to see the benefits of war but be blind to its costs.

Legitimate (Proper) Authority
In contrast to the other principles, this one has not until recently been particularly contentious. Now there is the issue of the UN overriding national authorities in certain circumstances. It often seems that overriding is acceptable to a nation when the votes in the UN is projected to be favourable to that nation. If the vote promises not to be favourable, then the talk turns to national inviolability and the UN is forgotten.

IN BELLO *PRINCIPLES*

Proportionality
It is no doubt easier to assess the costs and benefits of a battle or campaign than it is in the whole war. But because battles are so unpredictable, assessments prior to the start of a battle are still not easy to make, and will vary wildly.

Discrimination
The variation of circumstances will dictate what the Rules of Engagement are. Inevitably, there will be disagreements about how these rules are to be written. As a war gets more serious for a nation – as it did in 1940 for Britain – the Rules of Engagement may allow targeting of people and places not allowable when victory is in sight. What should be allowed during a war that is going seriously wrong for a nation can be debated endlessly.

These loose features could be citied by almost any critic of JWT. Realists are in a position to say that looseness encourages defenders of JWT to pursue all sorts of foolish humanitarian military adventures. These critics can say further that just war theorists manipulate the theory until they get the war outcome they desire. But, more than likely, it is the pacifists who latch onto looseness as a very serious flaw in JWT.

There are, of course, many kinds of pacifists. There are nuclear pacifists who, as their name implies, are opposed unalterably to the use of nuclear weapons to start or fight a war. There are also personal pacifists who profess pacifism for themselves, but do not get seriously involved in altering government policies or in telling others whether they should go to war. Another form of personal pacifism 'disavows the use of force in defense of self while permitting, and even demanding, its employment in defense of the state'.[2] Among other types, there are also those who can be called universal or absolute pacifists, and they will be the focus of our attempt better to understand JWT. They are opposed to JWT because they oppose all wars and all forms of violence. For them all wars are immoral so there is no reason to make distinctions between 'good' and 'bad' wars.

Notice that if one holds a position like universal pacifism there is only room for a small amount of looseness in the theory. There will be some looseness, for example, when one wonders whether pushing someone back into an unruly crowd counts as an act of violence but this sort of looseness does not compare with that found in JWT. The looseness in that theory leads to a wide variety of divergent decisions. Pacifism doesn't suffer from that distemper: the theory tells its followers precisely what to do. They are not to take any steps to get themselves or their country involved in war. This certainty as to what is to be done comes from the theory's refusal to get into the business of making exceptions. There are no exceptions to the principle that nations shall not engage in violence when they have disagreements with one another. It is the business of how to make exceptions that gets theorists into trouble. If you grant that the no killing, violence, etc. rules have exceptions, trouble begins. Further, when one realizes how varied wars are as to: 1) their length; 2) where they are fought (e.g., in the mountains, urban areas); 3) the number of non-combatants near the fighting; 4) the kind of military equipment available; 5) the relative military strength of the contesting parties; 6) the number of nations and non-nation groups involved; and 7) the political nature of the governments or groups involved, the trouble caused by looseness is magnified.

The looseness is so great that pacifists can easily take advantage of it by pretending to be just war theorists. When last resort (see Chapter 3) comes up for consideration in a setting where war threatens, they can play the infinity game (see Chapter 10). They can argue for negotiations, more negotiations, sanctions, deadlines, still more negotiations, on to infinity. They can play games with the other principles as well. They can be so strict in applying the likelihood of success principle that they can claim there is little or no chance of being successful if one starts a war. By the calculations of our stealth pacifists, this war will have more bad consequences if started than good ones. Likewise with proportionality. The same conclusion applies to that war and that one too.

DEALING WITH LOOSENESS

So it cannot be denied that looseness, or what I earlier called plasticity, is found in JWT. But how damaging is looseness to the theory? Comparing pacifism to JWT, the latter cannot help but look damaged. If the strictness found in pacifism is the model of how theories in ethics work, the looseness found in JWT seems intolerable. It is tempting to think that if JWT can't control its looseness any better than it does at present, we ought to abandon it and forge, instead, a different way of dealing with the ethical problems posed by war.[3]

But a paradox needs to be dealt with before we can be accused of abandoning our child. On the one side, the looseness of JWT should make it impossible, or at least very difficult, for anyone to draw meaningful conclusions about the ethics of war. Yet on the other side, we found in Chapter 4 (concerning easy cases) that the theory can be used to good effect in rendering judgements about various aspects of World War II and the Korean War. The theory even seems to work with many of the not-so-easy cases discussed in Chapter 5. The paradox, then, is that the theory seems not to work when viewed one way, but apparently does work when viewed another way.

How to dispel the paradox? The process can start by turning again to the universal pacifist theory and coming to realize that the theory's strictness is atypical. Theories, or at least principles found in ethics, can be articulated so as to give us strictness comparable to that of pacifism. For example, a principle might simply tell us 'Don't kill your fellow humans'. Stated in such general terms it can accomodate exceptions. Smith might say that he accepts the principle, but allows that in war it need not be wrong to kill an enemy soldier. But the principle can be stated more precisely as follows: 'Don't ever intentionally kill innocent born or unborn children'. Now if one is tempted to kill an innocent unborn child, the principle will clearly give guidance not to do such a thing. Other rules or principles can be similarly articulated in a clear and unambiguous fashion: 'Don't ever tell lies to rational, fully conscious, wilful (i.e., autonomous) persons'.

However, the problem with this way of talking and thinking is proliferation: one would need a host of rules and principles to cover the waterfront, and even then there would be gaps in the coverage. For example, the fully articulated principles aren't necessarily going to tell you whether and when it is permissible to lie to those who are not fully rational.

Because it is difficult (to say the least) to formulate a system of rules and principles that are clear and precise, we are generally content to settle for less. We can see this less ambitious way of thinking at work in the law. Legislators pass laws where they attempt to speak in a clear and precise voice. By doing so it is possible for some laws in some situations to be applied directly from the 'black letter law'. As the facts emerge, it is clear that Joe has killed his partner in crime so that he could have all the money they stole from the bank. Once Joe is caught, and once the police discover what happened, the court can deal with Joe with dispatch. But there are other cases where the law does not speak with a clear voice.[4] Suzy was encouraged to engage in crime, but Joe didn't just encourage her, he said that if she did not help pull off the heist, he would leave her to care for her future child all by herself. If, in fact, Suzy helps Joe, and is later caught by the police, how should she be treated? Was she coerced and thus less guilty of committing a crime than Joe? The 'black letter law' doesn't necessarily tell us how to deal with her the same way that it tells us how to deal with Joe. What it advises us to do is to keep in mind the law that forbids heists, but to determine Suzy's level of complicity in court where a jury can reach a verdict.

Much the same point can be made by relating a story from the American Civil War. Evidently the commander-in-chief of the Southern forces, General Robert E. Lee, was accustomed to giving 'loose' orders.[5] He did not specify in great detail what he wanted his commanders to do. In effect, he gave them discretion to deal with problems as they might develop in the field. When his second in command was General 'Stonewall' (Thomas J.) Jackson, this policy worked well: Jackson acted with style and decisiveness, and tended to behave in ways that Lee would have approved of. Unfortunately, Jackson was killed accidentally by his own troops fairly early in the war. He was replaced by the competent but perhaps less secure Lieutenant General Richard S. Ewell. Ewell did not live well with 'loose' orders. He wanted Lee to tell him precisely what he was supposed to do. When he received an order from Lee, Ewell typically fretted and complained. Worse still, because he wasn't sure what his commander wanted him to do, he hesitated when it would have been better for him to act decisively. His hesitancy turned out to be costly in the great battle at Gettysburg.[6] Rather than move decisively to take Cemetery Hill, a key objective in the battle, he waited for more troops to come on line. By then it was too late.

Of course, Lee could have given more precise orders and made Ewell feel secure. But consider two reasons why he might not have wanted to do so. First, he might have realized that it is impossible in certain situations to give completely specific instructions. Second, even if his instructions could be completely specific, he might not have wanted Ewell to implement them because the situation might have changed from the time of issuance to that of implementation. A rigid rule-following Ewell would have likely carried out Lee's specific orders even if they were no longer applicable to the situation. Better, then, to keep things 'loose' and allow a smart commander like Jackson to do the right thing at the right time in the right way. To be sure, there might have been times when more specific orders than those Lee commonly gave were called for. But, the point is, at other times such orders might not be called for.

The lesson of these examples is as follows. It is not a fatal flaw of JWT that it contains looseness. That looseness does not prevent applying the theory directly to certain situations. Once we gather the relevant facts, it tells us who in 1939 was the aggressor in Poland. But the looseness also encourages those who use the theory in many situations to treat its principles as rough guidelines. The users, then, are expected to interpret the theory in such a way as to allow them to make specific judgements about their specific situation. They are thus expected not just to read answers directly off of the theory, but to engage in some critical thinking about the situation they are facing.

That sort of thinking is needed for another reason when using JWT. As was made clear in the discussion of just cause in Chapter 6, the theory is open-ended: it isn't as if the six classic good reasons for going to war represent a complete list. There are too many good reasons out in the real world to allow for completeness so that, for example, aggression can be understood simply as border crossing. So critical thinking is needed not just to interpret already stated principles, but also to help supplement these principles.

TECHNOLOGY

Looseness, some claim, is a reason for abandoning Just War Theory. I have argued against that claim. JWT is certainly loose, but the theory can be used in making a wide variety of decisions about war in spite of this defect. So the theory should not be abandoned on that account. However, another argument has been cited for abandoning JWT, one totally different from those discussed so far. It is a recent argument, which came to the fore as weapons technology continued to develop, and do so at an accelerating pace, after World War II.

The argument takes many forms. In the 1950s through the 1980s the dominant form focused on nuclear weapons. These weapons, it was said, make war impossible.[7] There is no way that JWT can be applied because, for one, there is no likelihood of success when nuclear weapons are tossed around by both sides: both are losers.

Starting in the 1980s, perhaps even before then, the argument was extended so as to apply to a variety of other modern weapons. Attention was given to so-called fuel-air bombs that release a flammable mist above the ground soon after being dropped from an airplane.[8] The resulting explosion resembles a small nuclear bomb. Attention was also given to cluster bombs. When they are released these bombs break up into hundreds of bomblets that wreak havoc over a large area. But it wasn't just that new area weapons were being fielded. Ordinary bombs were getting smaller but more powerful. On the ground, automatic weapons were put in the hands of every soldier. The sheer firepower of the new rifles along with machineguns was overwhelming.

The revolution in weapons was not restricted to their disabling function; they also had a greater reach than before.[9] Airplanes came to fly across oceans sometimes at supersonic speeds. Missiles flew even faster, and also had an intercontinental reach. Then helicopters came on line after World War II. Soon they were armed with machineguns, cannon and rockets. They could also be used, and were used, to ferry troops behind enemy lines. Helicopters thus helped turn the battlefield from one where enemies faced one another at a front line into a fluid affair where the fighting could take place over hundreds of square miles on either side of what used to be the front line. Artillery increased both its reach and intensity. Using rockets, missiles and modern cannon, the enemy could now be attacked at least twice as deep as before, and with much greater accuracy.

As if that was not enough, modern weaponry was radically improved in its locating function.[10] By using sophisticated radar, thermal imaging devices, light enhancing equipment and so on, war became a 24-hour, all seasons and all weather affair. With weapons that could locate one's enemies no matter where they are hiding, that could reach them no matter how far away they are and then disable them completely, war was getting to look so fierce that it seemed it no longer belonged within the ethical realm. It was just too easy to kill in the twentieth and twenty-first centuries for JWT to have any role to play any longer.

As with so many of the criticisms of JWT discussed already, this one too makes a valid point. If all these modern weapons were deployed in a war like the one that could have taken place in the 1970s and 1980s between the USSR and its allies and the USA and its allies, everyone would have been a loser. A war like that would probably have been not much different from one using nuclear weapons. If war in the future has to be like this, we should all abandon JWT and turn into pacifists.

Wars, however, don't have to be conceived that way. Lesser wars between nations and wars between nations and non-nation groups can still deliver winners and losers. Indeed wars can and are being fought that leave survivors on both the winning and losing side. One reason this can happen is that some of the new weapons deployed make JWT more rather than less viable. These weapons, the smart ones, make it possible to appeal to the discrimination principle to a degree that was impossible 50 years ago. Today a modern jet can locate a bridge precisely, reach that bridge without even flying over it, and then destroy it with one missile. No longer need an air force drop scores of bombs on the bridge (and accidentally on the village nearby) to destroy it; today it can be done with one bomb and near-zero collateral damage.

So the argument appealing to technology does not destroy Just War Theory. There are different kinds of wars in the world and some of them can still be judged by using the theory.

BACK TO THE TWIN THEORY

One more problem with the theory needs to be examined. It is a different sort of problem from those already discussed in this and the previous chapter, because it is not concerned with JWT in general but with the particular version of the theory presented in Chapter 9. In that chapter, one theory was turned into two theories. One was for so called regular wars between nations (JWT-R), the other was for irregular war between nations and non-nation groups (JWT-I).

The problem facing the twin version of JWT has to do with choice. Since wars don't always divide neatly into the categories of regular and irregular, it is at times difficult to know which theory one is supposed to choose in order to weigh the ethical dilemmas of the participants. If there is no way to decide which theory to invoke, that might lead to confusion – especially if each side in a struggle chooses differently.

No doubt, for most wars, there is no problem: everyone can name scores of wars that fall under JWT-R. Everyone can also (perhaps with a little effort) identify scores of irregular wars. So the wars that might pose a problem of choice are not going to be overly large in number but they will be a varied lot, so it is worth examining two examples to see exactly how they should be handled.

Consider first the US Civil War (1861–65). The war could be thought of as one involving a large group of loosely organized rebels who wanted to secede from the union. In that way of thinking, rebel efforts would fall under the irregular model of JWT, so the rebels would not have to identify a legitimate authority in their attempt at secession. Nor would they have to make a likelihood of success assessment, although they would have to satisfy the other criteria.

However, when one notes that those who seceded were up until then *states* of the union, and not just rebel groups, their actions begin to look more like regular war. The state of South Carolina was the first to secede on 20 December 1860. It was followed quickly by six other states. By February 1861, the rebel states banded together to form a provisional government, the Confederate States of America. So even before the war got underway, the war-to-be was between two governments: one a fully-fledged state, the other a nation in the making. Assessment of the war in terms of JWT thus clearly falls under the regular rather than the irregular model.

In contrast, it is more difficult to place the American Revolutionary War under one or the other model. Discontent among the colonists was in place long before the war started.[11] Much of the discontent had to do with taxation. Evidently the British government was under pressure to raise taxes wherever it could in the Empire to help support its worldwide policies of military and economic expansion. Bridling against taxes that were imposed without representation, the colonists began drifting towards war. They boycotted tea (one of the taxed items), kept ships laden with tea from landing on American shores, goaded British soldiers into killing citizens (the Boston Massacre) and fought the British at Lexington and Concord (19 April 1775).

These and other events took place before serious steps were taken to form an overall government to sponsor the revolution. One step had in fact taken place earlier. On 5 September 1774 the colonists had formed a Continental Congress to oppose British tax policies but it wasn't until 15 June the following year that George Washington was appointed commander-in-chief by the Congress, and not until 1776 that the colonists declared their independence.

So the war started with and without a government in place. Some of the events leading to war were authorized by the Congress while others were not. Which version of JWT, then, is one to invoke to assess this and similar wars? There are four possible answers. Invoke one version of the theory, invoke the other, both, or neither. In effect, the latter invocation gives up on JWT. That is an option to be taken only after making a final, and negative, assessment of JWT. So for now that option will be set aside.

What about invoking the regular version of JWT? If this were done by giving the colonists the benefit of the doubt concerning their government being in place, then they would be assessed in the same way that any other people with a government would be. So, for example, if the Continental Congress had authorized the revolution to begin (even though the war had in certain ways started already), then that authorization would count as legitimate. That seems fair enough to the colonists, although the British might have argued that the revolutionaries should not have been given the benefit of the doubt as having the status of a legitimate government.

But following British preferences would mean moving to the irregular version in order to make an assessment of the revolution. That move would not be terribly unfair to the revolutionaries either. Like appealing to the regular version, the colonists would have to satisfy just cause, and also have good intentions, proportionality and last resort on their side. However, they would not have to meet the standards of legitimate authority and likelihood of success principles.

In truth, the British would not have gained much by moving from the regular to the irregular version. This is because their appeal to JWT would not rest on the choice of one or the other of the two versions of JWT; rather, it probably rests on an appeal to just cause and last resort. They would likely have argued that the colonists did not have just cause for going to war and also that they had not exhausted all of the resorts available to them for avoiding war.

If it doesn't make any difference to either side which option is chosen, the question arises: why bother to develop two versions of JWT? The answer here comes in two parts. First, we should not expect that one side or the other would be favoured by this or that version. The versions of JWT are not put in place to privilege one side's justification process at the expense of the other side. Rather, second, they are put in place in order to facilitate the thinking process. Irregular wars are different enough from regular ones to require different principles. If, however, a war comes along where it is difficult to decide whether its nature is regular or irregular, we have found that to be problematic and, as yet, we have found no satisfactory way of dealing with the problem.

But there is a way. If, like the American colonial situation, the war moves haphazardly from being irregular to regular, it makes sense to appeal serially to both versions of JWT. When the war is mainly fought by an almost random collection of revolutionary groups, or even run by mobs that gather spontaneously in the streets, then those who think seriously about war should cite the irregular version of JWT. In theory, this citing might justify the war that is just starting or it might not justify it. Hopefully, this thinking might help end the conflict should the justification process show that the conflict is not justified. Or, if it fails to do that, it would restrain the nature of the fighting by honouring such principles as discrimination.

But once the rebel movement has taken political shape, either as the result of violence or other means of protest, then a second appeal to JWT is in order. The newly-formed government can now appeal to the regular version of JWT. Again, it might in theory find in favour of continuing the war or not. This point could be expressed differently: it might find in favour of starting the war *officially* or not. However it is expressed, this second ethical review of the situation might introduce additional restraints on war and for that reason do some good. In any case, it should be clear that there is nothing contradictory about appealing to both versions of JWT.

It would appear, then, that the problem of choice is not a serious one for Just War Theory. For most wars it will be clear which version of JWT should be chosen. On those rare occasions when the choice is difficult, both versions can be chosen. If the war starts out in a rag-tag fashion and then becomes more organized, then the irregular version will be chosen first and the regular version later. If the war starts out as one between two nation states and then moves to the status of guerrilla war, then the regular version should be citied first and the irregular one later.

12 Closing Thoughts

Just War Theory is bleeding, but not bleeding to death. The bleeding results from underuse, from the theory being used as window dressing, from the harm it does when it is used and from how loose (plastic) it is. Further bleeding results from modern warfare with its overwhelmingly powerful killing machines. Such warfare seems to make Just War Theory obsolete. All this bleeding has been looked at and judged not to be fatal. Rigidity is another cause of bleeding, although it has not been talked of as such. Defenders of the theory tend to treat it as if it is rigidly fixed in place by tradition, by reason, by logic or what have you. One result is that when they apply it to modern wars and war-like situations, the theory's defenders find the applications difficult. They then become discouraged and so come to feel that their theory should, after all, be put to sleep.

This study claims that it is not time to put the theory in its final resting place. It is, however, time for changes which correspond with how war has changed. Not everything needs changing. Basic principles of JWT such as just cause must be kept in place simply because wars represent exceptions to ethical rules; and good reasons (just causes) are needed to explain why the exceptions should be permitted. But much will change. The most important change is to turn Just War Theory into Just War Theories – two of them. One version is for regular wars between nations (JWT-R), the other for varied types of irregular struggles ('wars') between nations and non-nation groups (JWT-I). The most basic difference between the two versions is that the former applies the principles of the theory symmetrically, while the latter applies some of its principles asymmetrically. With symmetrical application both sides follow the same principles, that is, both are expected to meet the same standards in starting wars and in fighting them. With asymmetrical application, one side has to meet certain standards, but the other side does not.

Asymmetry seems unfair. Both sides, the thought is, ought to be playing by the same rules. But I have argued that this is impossible. Typically, the situations in which non-nation groups face the prospect and the reality of 'war' differ drastically from what nations have to face. Nations possess technology, money and political structure; non-nation groups usually have these goods in significantly lesser quantities. JWT-I reflects these differences by giving non-nation groups certain advantages. These groups do not have to meet the likelihood of success and legitimate authority standards. But the advantages do not accrue all to one side. Nations have the advantage with respect to the just cause and last resort principles. Unlike wars between nations where preventive strikes are (still) not permitted, such strikes are permitted in certain circumstances in 'wars' between nations and non-nation groups. So the alleged unfairness to one side or the other isn't all it seems.

With two versions of JWT in place to help deal with the variety of war and war-like activity, it makes sense to ask: just how much can be accomplished by JWT? Put differently, how much more can be done with the modified model of JWT than could be done with the standard model?

Looking at it one way, the gain is minimal. Whichever version is used, JWT cannot always deliver definitive answers to the ethical questions that disturb us about war. The main reason it cannot is that the theory deals with exceptions. No matter how the theory is fashioned, dealing with exceptions to standard rules and principles often puts us face-to-face with serious conflict situations. Some of these situations are not easily, or not ever, resolvable.

Even assuming that we have all the relevant facts to help us make a decision, the pros and cons of going to war with our enemy tomorrow may simply balance out. Having a theory in hand is not going to change the balance sheet. But facts aside, the looseness of JWT (really almost any theory) will prevent those who use it from generating definitive answers to the questions they have asked themselves.

Clearly, then, theories can't do everything. Even if we employ flawless logic in our thinking about war, the nature of the conflict itself (it is often a close call), the shortage of information and the looseness of the JWT principles will all prevent those who use the theory from always coming to agreement.

When there is no agreement it will seem that appealing to the theory is a waste of time. But it isn't. It may be a disappointment, but it isn't a waste for several reasons. The first is that appealing to the theory, to logic and to the facts of a war situation forces those who are thinking about it to articulate more clearly what their stance on that war is. They themselves will come better to understand their stance. The process may even alter their stance somewhat, soften or harden it, even if it does not change it in any fundamental way. Second, if the theory is articulated publicly, others will understand the stance better. Third, in advance of using the theory, our various thinkers, both inside and outside government, will not know whether they will come to some agreement or not. To the surprise of everyone, using the theory may lead to agreement. Fourth, the theory is useful for retrospective analysis. After a war has been over for some time, heads become somewhat cooler. The analysis never becomes completely dispassionate, but it is usually less guided by the fiery emotions common as a war is about to begin and, once it has begun, as stories of atrocities get reported (and misreported). With cooler heads, it becomes possible to learn lessons from what has happened.

So Just War Theory has uses even when disagreement abounds. Of course, it will have uses as well where there is at least some agreement. But quite apart from how much agreement is present, there are additional reasons for supposing that Just War Theory will not, and should not, be abandoned. I will mention two.

First, the greater destructive power of modern weapons does not necessarily mean that war is impossible ethically. Some of the new 'smart' weapons make it possible to adhere to the principle of discrimination at a level undreamed of even as late as the Vietnam War. There will always be collateral damage, especially if one side chooses to fight in urban centres. But with smart weapons that damage can be, and often is, much less than it would have been with the technology of the past. Further, the pressure on nations with the means to develop and deploy these weapons actually to use them will increase in the future. These weapons are fully accepted in military and political circles so a nation cannot easily excuse itself when it fails to deploy and use them.

Second, the mass media will prevent JWT from being abandoned, because it 'sees all and reports all', or perhaps it is better to say that it 'sees most things and reports most things'. However one puts it, the mass media have changed war forever. No longer is it possible to engage in war and violate either the proportionality principle or the discrimination principle and not get 'caught'. Put differently, developments in the mass media have helped turn things around for JWT. The theory today is more, rather than less, relevant than it was one or two generations ago.

These considerations concerned with JWT's survival in the modern world lead to the conclusion that the theory is (still) alive even if it is not well. Its illness is not fatal or near to being fatal. Rather, the theory is alive and recovering. We have reason to believe that it will continue to recover.

Notes

Chapter 1

1. On many occasions 'principles' and 'rules' can be used interchangeably. This is because principles are rules, although not all rules are principles. When the two terms differ it is because 'principles' refers to rules that are more basic or fundamental. Unfortunately these terms are vague so that what is to one thinker a principle is a rule to another.
2. The list looks very much like the one W. D. Ross gave us many years ago in his *The Right and the Good* (Oxford: Clarendon Press, 1930), p. 21.
3. *Ibid.*, p. 19. Ross suggest two other terms that could be used here: '*prima facie*' and 'conditional'.
4. Nick Fotion and Jenifer H. Tai, 'Applying Just Medical Theory', *Philosophical Inquiry*, XXIV (1–2), Winter–Spring, 2002: 29–42.
5. R. M. Hare, *Moral Thinking: Its Levels, Method and Point* (Oxford: Clarendon Press, 1981), pp. 25–41.
6. Nicholas Wade, 'Korean Scientist Said to Admit Fabrication in a Cloning Study', *The New York Times*, 16 December 2005, pp. A1, A6. See also, in the same issue, a commentary by Gina Kolada, 'Clone Scandal: "A Tragic Turn" for Science', p. A6.

Chapter 2

1. Confucius, *The Analects* (London: Penguin Books, 1970), bk. 12, ch. 7; bk. 13, chs. 29–30; bk. 16, ch. 1.

2. Mencius, *The Works of Mencius*, bk. 1, pt. 1, chs. 4–7; pt. 2, ch. 8; bk. 2; pt. 1, chs. 2–3 in *Chinese Classics*, James Legge (ed.) (Oxford: Oxford University Press, 1894).
3. Mo Tzu, *Basic Writings*, trans. by Burton Watson (New York: Columbia University Press, 1963) pp. 50–61.
4. Plato, *The Republic*, trans. by B. Jowett (New York: The Modern Library), bk. II, 373e–374a; bk. V, 469b, 470.
5. Aristotle, *Nicomachean Ethics* (1177b6) in Richard McKeon (ed.), *The Basic Works of Aristotle* (New York: Random House, 1941).
6. *The Laws of Manu*, trans. by Wendy Doniger and Brian K. Smith (New York: Penguin, 1991), pp. 137–40. See also *The Bhagavad Gita*, trans. by Eliot Geutsch (New York: Holt, Rinehart and Winston, 1968).
7. Frederick H. Russell, *The Just War in the Middle Ages* (London: Cambridge University Press, 1975).
8. John Kelsay, *Islam and War: The Gulf War and Beyond* (Louisville, KY: Westminister/ John Knox Press, 1993), pp. 16–27.
9. Hugo Grotius, *The Laws of War and Peace*, trans. by Francis W. Kelsey (Indianapolis: Bobbs-Merrill, 1962).
10. The following is a sample of recent books published in this tradition: Paul Christopher, *The Ethics of War and Peace* (Englewood Cliffs, NJ: Prentice Hall Inc., 1994); A. J. Coates, *The Ethics of War* (Manchester and New York: Manchester University Press, 1997); Shelton Cohen, *Arms and Judgment: Law, Morality and the Conduct of War in the Twentieth Century* (Boulder and London: Westview Press, 1989); James Turner Johnson, *Just War Tradition and the Restraint of War* (Princeton, NJ: Princeton University Press, 1981); Barrie Paskins, *The Ethics of War* (Minneapolis, MN: Minnesota University Press, 1979); Paul Ramsey, *War and the Christian Conscience* (Durham, NC: Duke University Press, 1961); Malham M. Wakin (ed.), *War, Morality and the Military Profession* (2nd edn.; Boulder and London: Westview Press, 1986); Michael Walzer, *Just and Unjust Wars* (New York: Basic Books, 1977).
11. Mo Tzu, *op. cit.*, 50–61.
12. John Rawls, *The Law of Peoples* (Cambridge, MA and London: Harvard University Press), 1999 pp. 36–7.
13. A series of articles appeared on this topic in the *Journal of Military Ethics*, 5 (2), 2006: Kenneth Roth, 'Was the Iraq War a Humanitarian

Intervention?', pp. 84–92; Fernando R. Teson, 'Eight Principles for Humanitarian Intervention', pp. 93–113; James Turner Johnson, 'Humanitarian Intervention after Iraq: Just War and International Law', pp. 114–27; James Muldoon, 'Francisco De Vitoria and Humanitarian Intervention', pp. 128–43; Alex J. Bellamy and Paul D. Williams, 'The UN Security Council and the Question of Humanitarian Intervention in Darfur', pp. 144–60.

14. Carl Ceulemans, 'Just Cause', in Bruno Coppieters and Nick Fotion (eds), *Moral Constraints on War* (Lanham, Boulder, New York and Oxford: Lexington Books, 2002), pp. 29–30.
15. See Chapter 8 for a more detailed discussion of this distinction.
16. James F. Childress, 'Just-War Theories: The Bases, Interpretations, Priorities, and the Functions of Their Criteria', in Malham M. Wakin (ed.), *War, Morality and the Military Profession* (Boulder and London: Westview Press, 1986), p. 264. See also A. J. Coates, 'Last Resort', in A. J. Coates (ed.), *The Ethics of War* (Manchester and New York: Manchester University Press, 1997), pp. 189–208.
17. Nick Fotion, 'Proportionality', in Bruno Coppieters and Nick Fotion (eds), *Moral Constraints on War* (Lanham, Boulder, New York and London: Lexington Books, 2002), pp. 91–9.
18. Nick Fotion and Bruno Coppieters, 'Likelihood of Success,' in *ibid.*, pp. 79–90.
19. Bruno Coppieters and Boris Kashnikov, 'Right Intentions', in *ibid.*, *Moral Constraints on War* pp. 59–77.
20. A. J. Coates, 'Legitimate Authority', in A. J. Coates (ed.), *The Ethics of War*, pp. 123–45.
21. Thomas L. Friedman, 'The Kidnapping of Democracy', in *The New York Times*, 14 July 2006, p. A 19. Friedman's argument is that minority groups such as Hezbollah are trying to influence politics in Lebanon in many ways, including moving that country in the direction of war. If they were to succeed, the war they start would not be legitimately authorized.
22. Guy Van Damme and Nick Fotion, 'Proportionality', in *Moral Constraints on War*, pp. 129–39.
23. Anthony Hartle, 'Discrimination', in *ibid.*, pp. 141–58.

Chapter 3

1. A. J. Coates, 'Pacifism', in *The Ethics of War*, pp. 77–96. See also Nick Fotion, Bruno Coppieters and Ruben Apressyan, 'Introduction: Pacifism', in *Moral Constraints on War*, pp. 7–10.
2. E. H. Carr, *The Twenty Years of Crisis, 1919–1939* (London: Macmillan, 1981).
3. Mark Evans, 'Moral Theory and the Idea of a Just War', in Mark Evans (ed.), *Just War Theory: A Reappraisal* (Edinburgh: Edinburgh University Press, 2005), pp. 11–12.
4. Michael R. Gordon and Bernard E. Trainor, *The Generals' War* (Boston, New York, Toronto and London: Little, Brown, 1995), pp. 136–8.
5. *Ibid.*, p. 136.
6. *Ibid.*, pp. 340–1.
7. Anthony Lewis, 'Making Torture Legal', *The New York Review of Books*, July 15, 2004, 4, 6, 8.
8. John F. Burns, 'Getting Used To War As Hell', *The New York Times*, 4 June 2006, section 4, 1, 4.
9. Hassam M. Fattah, 'As Lebanon's Fuel Runs Out, Fears of a Doomsday Moment', *The New York Times*, 9 August, 2006, p. A11. On the same page see John Fifner, 'Israel Warns Lebanese It Will Bomb Vehicles in the South'. These two reports are typical of what one reads every day.

Chapter 4

1. Gerhard L. Weinberg, *A World at Arms: A Global History of World War II* (Cambridge: Cambridge University Press, 1994), p. 37.
2. *Ibid.*, pp. 34–5.
3. *Ibid.*, p. 32.
4. *Ibid.*, p. 32.
5. B. H. Liddell Hart, *The History of the Second World War* (New York: Putnam, 1970), p. 133.
6. Williamson Murray and Allan R. Millett, *A War to Be Won: Fighting the Second World War* (Cambridge, MA.: The Belknap Press, 2000), p. 103.
7. *Ibid.*, p. 104.
8. I. C. B. Dear (ed.), *The Oxford Companion to World War II* (Oxford: Oxford University Press, 1995), p. 504.

9. Murray and Millett, *op. cit.*, pp. 119–20.
10. Weinberg, *op. cit.*, p. 267.
11. Murray and Millett, *op. cit.*, pp. 146–7.
12. Dear, *op. cit.*, p. 216.
13. Murray and Millett, *op. cit.*, p. 160.
14. *Ibid.*, p. 164.
15. Hart, *op. cit.*, p. 199.
16. Murray and Millett, *op. cit.*, p. 176.
17. The video entitled *Murder Under the Sun: Japanese War Crimes and Trials*, produced by Lou Reda, vividly portrays many of the Japanese violations of the discrimination principle (Lou Reda Productions, in association with The National Historical Society, 1996).
18. Michael Russell, *Iwo Jima* (New York: Random, 1974), pp. 144, 147.
19. Hart, *op. cit.*, p. 690.
20. Weinberg, *op. cit.*, p. 870.
21. Because they raise so many new questions, the atomic bomb attacks on Hiroshima and Nagasaki are not brought into the assessment of the American bombing campaign on Japan. In brief, however, the following can be said. The principles of discrimination and proportionality can, at times, come into conflict. If the former is taken as the dominant principle in this conflict, then the bombings have to be condemned as immoral. If the proportionality principle is dominant, then rare exceptions to discrimination are allowed. Indeed, some have argued that exceptions should be allowed in these twin bombings. Why? Because an invasion of Japan would have been several times more costly to the Americans (and their allies) and to the Japanese than the bombings in fact turned out to be to the Japanese.
22. Stanley Sandler, *The Korean War: No Victor, No Vanquished* (Lexington: The University Press of Kentucky, 1999), pp. 37–41.
23. *Ibid.*, p. 40.
24. *Ibid.*, pp. 28–31.
25. *Ibid.*, p. 45.
26. *Ibid.*, p. 42.
27. Roy K. Flint, 'Korean War: 1950–1953', an entry in John Whiteclay Chambers II *et al.* (eds), *American Military History* (Oxford: Oxford University Press, 1999), p. 369.
28. Sandler, *op. cit.*, pp. 54–9.

29. Callum A. MacDonald, *Korea: The War Before Vietnam* (New York: The Free Press, 1986), pp. 48–50.
30. Sandler, *op. cit.*, pp. 85–93.
31. *Ibid.*, pp. 59–60.
32. *Ibid.*, pp. 37–8.
33. MacDonald, *op. cit.*, p. 210.
34. *Ibid.*, pp. 233–46.

Chapter 5

1. A. J. P. Taylor, *A History of the First World War* (New York: George Rainbird Limited, 1963, 1966), p. 15.
2. John Keegan, *The First World War* (New York: Alfred A. Knopf, 1999), p. 49.
3. A. J. P. Taylor, *op. cit.*, pp. 9–13.
4. L.C.F. Turner, *Origins of the First World War* (New York: W. W. Norton, 1970), p. 79.
5. Hew Strachan, *The First World War* (New York, Toronto, London, etc.: Penguin Books, 2005), pp. 3–10.
6. Turner, *op. cit.*, p. 88.
7. *Ibid.*, pp. 91–111.
8. *Ibid.*, p. 110.
9. Keegan, *op. cit.*, p. 64.
10. Turner, *op. cit.*, pp. 96, 104, 108.
11. Carl Ceulemans, 'The NATO Intervention in the Kosovo Crisis', in Bruno Coppieters and Nick Fotion (eds), *Moral Constraints on War*, p. 205.
12. Ivo H. Daalder and Michael E. O'Hanlon, *Winning Ugly: NATO's War to Save Kosovo* (Washington, DC: Brookings Institution Press, 2000), p. 12.
13. *Ibid.*, p. 212.
14. Human Rights News, 'Human Rights Watch investigation Finds Yugoslav Forces Guilty of War Crimes in Racak, Kosovo', http://hrw.org/english/docs/1999/01/29/serbia756.htm. Accessed 15 December 2005.
15. *Ibid.*
16. Boris Kashnikov, 'NATO's Intervention in the Kosovo Crisis: Whose Justice?', in *Moral Contstraints on War*, pp. 242–3.
17. John Keegan, *The Iraq War* (New York: Vintage Books, 2005), p. 110.

18. *Ibid.*, pp. 110–14. See also Todd S. Purdum, *A Time of Our Choosing: America's War in Iraq* (New York: Times Books, 2003), pp. 46–62.

Chapter 6

1. Mo Tzu, *Basic Writings* (New York: Columbia University Press, 1963), pp. 52–61.
2. Franz J. Gayl, 'Electronic Chaos', in *US Naval Institute Proceedings*, December 2005, pp. 55–6. In the same issue see also 'America the Vulnerable' by Carl Weldon and Roscoe Bartlett, p. 57.

Chapter 7

1. *Wikepedia*, Fulgencio Batista, http://en.wikipedia.org/wiki/Fulgenio_Batista#Second_rule. Accessed 28 March 2007.
2. Sebastian Balfour, *Castro* (London: Longman, 1990), pp. 38–40.
3. *Ibid.*, pp. 47–8.
4. *Ibid.*
5. Carl Ceulemans, 'The Military Response of the US-led Coalition to the September 11 Attacks', in *Moral Constraints on War*, pp. 266–8.
6 Norman Friedman, *Terrorism, Afghanistan and America's New Way of War* (Annapolis, MO: Naval Instute Press, 2003), pp. 157–228.

Chapter 8

1. Neta C. Crawford, 'The Justice of Preemption and Preventive War Doctrines', in Mark Evans (ed.), *Just War Theory: A Reappraisal* (Edinburgh: Edinburgh University Press, 2005), pp. 25–49.
2. http://en.wikipedia.org/wiki/Ethnic_conflict_in_Sri_Lanka, accessed 15 May 2006.
3. Robert A. Pape, *Dying to Win: The Strategic Logic of Suicide Terrorism* (New York: Random House, 2005), p. 141.
4. Shimali Senana Yake, 'Pakistan's Envoy Nearly Killed in Sri Lanka', *The New York Times*, 15 August 2006, p. A6.
5. *Ibid.*

6. Kazi Mahmood, 'Thailand Perpetuating the Taming of Islam in Patani', 13 March 2002, http://www.islam-online.net/English/views/2002/03/article9shtml, accessed 6 June 2006.
7. Jeff Moore, 'Islamic Insurgency Run Amok', *US Naval Institute Proceedings*, May 2006, p. 39.
8. *Ibid.*, p. 40.
9. Tom Shanker, 'A New Enemy Gains On The US', *The New York Times*, section 4, 30 July 2006, p. 14.
10. Philip Shenon and Neil A. Lewis, 'Tracing Terror Plots, British Watch, Then Pounce', *The New York Times*, 13 August, 2006, 1, p. 4.
11. Norman Friedman, 'The Case for Pre-Emption', in *US Naval Institute Proceedings*, August 2006, pp. 90–91. Interestingly enough, Friedman does not make the distinction between preemption and prevention. He uses 'preemption' broadly to cover both concepts.

Chapter 9

1. Everett W. Hall, *Modern Science and Human Values* (Princeton, NJ: D. Van Nostrand Company, Inc., 1956), pp. 115–26.

Chapter 10

1. Nick Fotion, 'Reactions to War: Pacifism, Realism, and Just War Theory', in Andrew Valls (ed.), *Ethics in International Affairs* (Lanham, Boulder: Rowman & Littlefield, 2000) pp. 18–19.
2. Peter W. Galbraith, 'Mindless in Iraq', *The New York Review of Books*, LIII (13), 10 August 2006, pp. 28–31.
3. Carl Ceulemans, 'The NATO Intervention in the Kosovo Crisis: March–June 1999', in *Moral Constraints on War*, p. 206.
4. E. H. Carr, *The Twenty Years of Crisis*.
5. John Kifner, 'Israel is Powerful, Yes. But Not So Invincible', *The New York Times*, section 4, 30 July 2006, pp. 1, 14.
6. Ceulemans, *op. cit.*, pp. 222–4.
7. A. J. Coates, *The Ethics of War*, p. 22.

8. Newton Garver, 'Pacifism,' in Lawrence C. Becker and Charlotte B. Becker (eds), *Encyclopedia of Ethics* Vol. II (New York and London: Garland Publishing, Inc. 1992), pp. 925–7.

Chapter 11

1. Hugo Grotius, *The Law of War and Peace* (tran. Francis W. Kelsey; New York: Transnational Publishers, 1985), chapter 22, XVII, 2, p. 556.
2. A. J. Coates, *The Ethics of War*, p. 78.
3. G. Zahn, 'Pacifism and Just War Theory', in *Catholics and Nuclear War*, ed. by P. Murnion (London: Geoffrey Chapman, 1983), p. 110.
4. H. L. A. Hart, *The Concept of Law* (Oxford: Oxford University Press, 1961), pp. 121–32. Hart speaks of the open texture of law instead of its looseness.
5. Robert L. Swain, 'Generals at Odds', in *Military History*, July/August 2006, pp. 38–45.
6. *Ibid.*, p. 44.
7. Robert L. Holmes, *On War and Morality* (Princeton, NJ: Princeton University Press, 1989), pp. 214–59.
8. Nicholas G. Fotion, *Military Ethics: Looking Toward the Future* (Stanford, CA.: Hoover Institution Press, 1990), pp. 22–4.
9. *Ibid.*, pp. 19–22.
10. *Ibid.*, pp. 18–19.
11. Fred Anderson, 'Revolutionary War (1775–83): Causes', in John Whiteclay Chambers II *et al.* (eds), *American Military History* (Oxford: Oxford University Press, 1999), pp. 603–5.

Bibliography

Anderson, F. (1999), 'Revolutionary War (1775–83): Causes', in J. Whiteclay Chambers II *et al.* (eds), *American Military History*. Oxford: Oxford University Press.

Aristotle (1941), *Nicomachean Ethics*, in Richard McKeon (ed.), *The Basic Works of Aristotle*. New York: Random House.

Bellamy, A. J., Williams, P. D. (2006), 'The UN Security Council and the Question of Humanitarian Intervention in Darfur', *Journal of Military Ethics* 5 (2), pp. 144–60.

Bhagavad Gita, The (1968), E. Geutsch (trans). New York: Hold, Rinehart and Winston.

Burns, J. F. (2006), 'Getting Used to War as Hell', *The New York Times*, 4 June, 4 (1, 4).

Carr, E. H. (1981), *The Twenty Years of Crisis, 1919–1939*. London: Macmillan.

Ceulemans, C. (2002), 'Just Cause', in B. Coppieters and N. Fotion (eds), *Moral Constraints on War*. Lanham, Boulder, New York, Oxford: Lexington Books.

Ceulemans, C. (2002), 'The NATO Intervention in the Kosovo Crisis', in *Moral Constraints on War, op. cit*.

Ceulemans, C. (2002), 'The Military Response of the US-led Coalition to the September 11 Attacks', in *Moral Constraints on War, op. cit*.

Childress, J. (1986), 'Just-War Theories: The Bases, Interpretations, Priorities and Functions of Their Criteria', in M. Wakin (ed.), *War, Morality and the Military Profession*. Boulder, London: Westview Press.

Christopher, P. (1994), *The Ethics of War and Peace*. Englewood Cliffs, NJ: Prentice Hall Inc.

Confucius (1970), *The Analects*. London: Penguin Books.

Coates, A. J. (1997), *The Ethics of War*. Manchester: Manchester University Press.

Cohen, S. (1989), *Arms and Judgment: Law, Morality and the Conduct of War in the Twentieth Century*. Boulder, San Francisco, London: Westview Press.

Coppieters, B., Kashnikov , B. (2002), 'Right Intentions', in *Moral Constraints on War, op. cit.*

Crawford, N. (2005), 'The Justice of Preemption and Preventive War Doctrines', in M. Evans (ed.), *Just War Theory: A Reappraisal*. Edinburgh: Edinburgh University Press.

Daalder, I. H., O'Hanlon, M. E. (2000), *Winning Ugly: NATO's War to Save Kosovo*. Washington, DC: Brookings Institute Press.

Dear, I. C. B. (ed.) (1995), *The Oxford Companion to World War II*. Oxford, New York: Oxford University Press.

Fattah, H. M. (2006), 'As Lebanon's Fuel Runs Out, Fears of a Doomsday Moment', *The New York Times*, 9 August, A 11.

Fifner, J. (2006), 'Israel Warns Lebanese It Will Bomb Vehicles in the South', *The New York Times*, 9 August, A 11.

Flint, R. K. (1999), 'The Korean War, 1950–1953', in *American Military History, op. cit.*

Fotion, N. (1990), *Military Ethics: Looking Toward the Future*. Stanford, CA: Hoover Institution Press.

Fotion, N. (2000), 'Reaction to War: Pacifism, Realism, and Just War Theory', in A. Valls (ed.), *Ethics in International Affairs*. Lanham, Boulder, New York, London: Rowman & Littlefield.

Fotion, N., Tai, J. H. (2002), 'Applying Just Medical Theory', *Philosophical Inquiry* XXIV (1–2), pp. 29–42.

Fotion, N, Coppieters, B., Apressyan, R. (2002), 'Introduction: Pacifism', in *Moral Constraints on War, op. cit.*

Fotion, N. (2002), 'Proportionality', in *Moral Constraints on War, op. cit.*

Fotion, N., Coppieters, B. (2002), 'Likelihood of Success', in *Moral Constraints on War, op. cit.*

Friedman, N. (2003), *Terrorism, Afghanistan and America's New Way of War*. Annapolis, MD: Naval Institute Press.

Friedman, N. (2006), 'The Case for Pre-Emption', *US Naval Institute Proceedings*, August, pp. 90–1.

Friedman, T. (2006), 'The Kidnapping of Democracy', *The New York Times*, 14 July, A 19.

Galbraith, P. W. (2006), 'Mindless in Iraq', *The New York Review of Books*, LIII (13), 10 August.

Gayl, F. J. (2005), 'Electronic Chaos', *US Naval Institute Proceedings*, December, pp. 55–6.

Gordon, M, Trainor, B. E. (1995), *The Generals' War*. Boston, New York, Toronto, London: Little, Brown.

Grotius, H. (1962), *The Laws of War and Peace*, F.W. Kelsey (trans). Indianapolis: Bobbs-Merrill.

Hall, E. W. (1956), *Modern Science and Human Values*. Princeton, NJ, Toronto, London, New York: D. Van Nostrand Company.

Hare. R. M. (1981), *Moral Thinking: Its Levels, Method and Point*. Oxford: Clarendon Press.

Hart, H. L. A. (1961), *The Concept of Law*. Oxford: Oxford University Press.

Hartle, A. (2002), 'Discrimination', in *Moral Constraints on War, op. cit.*

Holmes, R. L. (1989), *On War and Morality*. Princeton, NJ: Princeton University Press.

Human Rights News (1999), 'Human Rights Watch Investigation Finds Yugoslav Forces Guilty of War Crimes in Racek, Kosovo', http://hrw.org/english/docs/1999/01/29/serbia756.htm.

Johnson, J. T. (1981), *Just War Tradition and the Restraint of War*. Princeton: Princeton University Press.

Johnson, J. T. (2006), 'Humanitarian Intervention after Iraq: Just War and International Law', *Journal of Military Ethics* 5 (2), pp. 114–27.

Kashnikov, B (2002), 'NATO's Intervention in the Kosovo Crisis: Whose Justice?', in *Moral Constraints on War, op. cit.*

Kelsay, J. (1993), *Islam and War: The Gulf War and Beyond*. Louisville: Westminister/John Knox Press.

Keegan, J. (1999), *The First World War*. New York: Alfred A. Knopf.

Keegan, J. (2005), *The Iraq War*. New York: Vintage Books.

Kifner, J. (2006), 'Israel is Powerful, Yes. But Not So Invincible', *The New York Times*, 30 July, 4 (1, 14).

Kolada, G. (2005), 'Clone Scandal: "A Tragic Turn" for Science', *The New York Times*, 16 December, A 6.

Lewis, A. (2004), 'Making Torture Legal', *The New York Review of Books*, 15 July, 4, 6, 8.

Liddell Hart, B. H. (1970), *The History of the Second World War*, New York: G. P. Putman's Sons.

MacDonald, C. A. (1986), *Korea: The War before Vietnam*. New York: The Free Press.

Mahmood, K. (2002), 'Thailand Perpetuating the Taming of Islam in Patani', http://www.islam-online.net/English/views/2002/03/article9shtml, accessed 15 August 2006.

Mencius (1894), *The Works of Mencius*, J. Legge (ed.), Oxford: Oxford University Press.

Manu, The Laws of (1968), W. Doniger and B. K. Smith (trans), New York: Penguin.

Moore, J. (2006), 'Islamic Insurgency Run Amok', *US Naval Institute Proceedings*, May, pp. 38–43.

Mo Tzu (1963), *Basic Writings*, B. Watson (trans). New York: Columbia University Press.

Muldoon, J. (2006), 'Francisco De Vitoria and Humanitarian Intervention', *Journal of Military Ethics*, 5 (2) 128–43.

Murray, W., Millett, A. R. (2000), *A War to be Won: Fighting the Second World War*, Cambridge, MA: Harvard University Press.

Pape, R. A. (2005), *Dying to Win: The Strategic Logic of Suicide Terrorism*. New York: Random House.

Paskins, B. (1979), *The Ethics of War*, Minneapolis. Minnesota University Press.

Plato (1928, 1956), *The Republic*, C. M. Bakewell (ed.); B. Jowett (trans). New York: The Modern Library.

Purdum, T. S. (2003), *A Time of Our Choosing: America's War in Iraq*. New York: Times Books.

Rawls, J. (1999), *The Law of Peoples*. Cambridge, MA: Harvard University Press.

Ramsey, P. (1961), *War and the Christian Conscience*. Durham, NC: Duke University Press.

Reda, L. (1996), *Murder under the Sun: Japanese War Crimes and Trials* (video). Lou Reda Productions in association with The National Historical Society.

Ross, W. D. (1930), *The Right and the Good*. Oxford, Clarendon Press.

Roth, K. (2006), 'Was the Iraq War a Humanitarian Intervention?', *Journal of Military Ethics*, 5 (2), pp. 84–92.

Russell, F. H. (1975), *The Just War in the Middle Ages*. London: Cambridge University Press.

Russell, M. (1974), *Iwo Jima*. New York: Random House.

Sandler, S. (1999), *The Korean War: No Victor, No Vanquished*. Lexington: The University Press of Kentucky.

Shanker, T. (2006), 'A New Enemy Gains On The US', *The New York Times,* 30 July, 4 (14).

Shenon, P., Lewis, N. A. (2006), 'Tracing Terror Plots, British Watch, Then Pounce', *The New York Times*, 13 August, 1, 4.

Strachan, H. (2005), *The First World War*. London: Penguin Books.

Swain, R. L. (2006), 'Generals at Odds', *Military History*, July/August.

Taylor, A. J. P. (1963, 1966), *A History of the First World War*. New York: George Rainbird.

Teson, F. R. (2006), 'Eight Principles for Humanitarian Intervention', *Journal of Military Ethics*, 5 (2), pp. 93–113.

Turner, L. C. F. (1970), *Origins of the First World War*. New York: W. W. Norton & Company Inc.

Wade, Nicholas (2005), 'Korean Scientist Said to Admit Fabrication in a Cloning Study', *The New York Times*, 16 December, A1, A6.

Van Damme G., Fotion, N. (2002), 'Proportionality (*in bello*)', in *Moral Constraints on War, op. cit*.

Walzer, M. (1977), *Just and Unjust Wars*. New York: Basic Books.

Weinberg, G. L. (1994), *A World at Arms: A Global History of World War II*. Cambridge: Cambridge University Press.

Weldon, C., Bartlett, R. (2005), 'America the Vulnerable', in *US Naval Institute Proceedings*, December, p. 57.

Yake, S. S. (2006), 'Pakistan's Envoy Nearly Killed in Sri Lanka', *The New York Times*, 15 August, A6.

Zahn, G. (1963), 'Pacifism and Just War Theory', in P. Murnion (ed.), *Catholics and Nuclear War*. London: Geoffrey Chapman.

Index